Enough Already!
Yes, You Are

A step-by-step guide to crushing the myth
that if you do just one more thing,
you will finally be enough

Elizabeth Trinkaus

Copyright © 2018 Elizabeth Trinkaus

Cover design: Mark Trinkaus of www.pentad.design
Back cover photo of Elizabeth by: Greg Fitts

All rights reserved. No part of this book may be used or reproduced by any means, graphic, electronic, or mechanical, including photocopying, recording, taping or by any information storage retrieval system without the written permission of the author except in the case of brief quotations embodied in critical articles and reviews.

Balboa Press books may be ordered through booksellers or by contacting:

Balboa Press
A Division of Hay House
1663 Liberty Drive
Bloomington, IN 47403
www.balboapress.com
1 (877) 407-4847

Because of the dynamic nature of the Internet, any web addresses or links contained in this book may have changed since publication and may no longer be valid. The views expressed in this work are solely those of the author and do not necessarily reflect the views of the publisher, and the publisher hereby disclaims any responsibility for them.

The author of this book does not dispense medical advice or prescribe the use of any technique as a form of treatment for physical, emotional, or medical problems without the advice of a physician, either directly or indirectly. The intent of the author is only to offer information of a general nature to help you in your quest for emotional and spiritual well-being. In the event you use any of the information in this book for yourself, which is your constitutional right, the author and the publisher assume no responsibility for your actions.

Any people depicted in stock imagery provided by Getty Images are models, and such images are being used for illustrative purposes only. Certain stock imagery © Getty Images.

Print information available on the last page.

ISBN: 978-1-9822-0302-3 (sc)
ISBN: 978-1-9822-0304-7 (hc)
ISBN: 978-1-9822-0303-0 (e)

Library of Congress Control Number: 2018905013

Balboa Press rev. date: 07/12/2018

Advance Praise
for
Enough Already! Yes, You Are

"With every personal and professional pursuit to achieve more, we are inevitably asked to give 'more.' Many of us do this without question, until we realize that we're dangerously close to burning out or thinking that our happiness is the cost of achieving our real potential. In other words, we just aren't enough! That's where the magic of this beautiful book comes to life. Written in an authentic voice and with a courageous mindset, we learn pure and powerful strategies to help us 'lean into' ourselves to find what's been there all along: our power to achieve and receive—to be our own catalyst for an infinite supply of more than 'enough.'"

—Dawn Galzerano, Senior Director, Cisco Systems

"*Enough Already! Yes, You Are* is an engaging and interactive collection of stories, lessons, tools, and exercises providing an illuminating path of support on your healing journey."

—Nancy Levin, Best-selling author of *The New Relationship Blueprint*

To the courageous souls who have been willing to examine their old stories and write new ones, knowing that the outcome of claiming ownership of their worth will forever illuminate their path. Shine on!

Contents

Introduction: Who This Book Is For xi

Chapter 1: We Teach What We Need to Learn 1
Chapter 2: Doubting Dotty and Believing Betty 9
Chapter 3: Statistically Speaking, You Really Are a Miracle 15
Chapter 4: 86 the Mirage 21
Chapter 5: Our Thoughts Affect Everything 25
Chapter 6: Switching the Station 29
Chapter 7: An Exercise Typically Reserved for the Dead 37
Chapter 8: The Courage to Affirm 41
Chapter 9: N-O-W 47
Chapter 10: My (Half) Marathon Story 51
Chapter 11: Choosing Love or Fear 57
Chapter 12: The Stories We Tell Ourselves 63
Chapter 13: Real-Life Clients' Old/New Stories 69
Chapter 14: Positive Chalk Talk 79
Chapter 15: The Backpack 81
Chapter 16: The Audacity to Shine 89
Chapter 17: Your Happy Place 99
Chapter 18: We All Need Reminders 103
Chapter 19: The *Enough Already!* Happy Dance 109

About the Author 111
Acknowledgments 113

Introduction

Who This Book Is For

This book is for the scholar, the surfer, the engineer, the unemployed; it's for the stay-at-home mom, the CEO, the dreamer, the retiree. It's for those who want to get *who* they are as something separate from *what* they have and do.

And, most importantly, it's for those who want to live with more joy and satisfaction TODAY. Not someday. Not after achieving this or acquiring that, not after that damn ship comes in . . .

For decades I have studied, counseled, and presented to thousands of people. The resounding message I've heard from clients is that happiness is out there somewhere, and if they just *do* more, *become* more, or try harder, they will arrive at *enough* . . . someday.

I myself have thought these thoughts and I have heard them with alarming frequency around me—so often, in fact, that I sometimes wonder if we have collectively been brainwashed to believe in a perpetual future but never in the *now*.

Well, *ENOUGH already*!! This pursuit of our "someday" has left us depleted, disillusioned, and depressed. It's time to turn this thing around. I'm here to crush the myth, to 86 the mirage—kick it to the curb—and give you multiple mind-bending tools that will have you experiencing deeper breaths and ah-ha moments.

And best of all, these tools will have you owning the joy elixir TODAY. Yes, today. Your new vision of yourself will have you here, NOW, living in the powerful present, with all of your perfect imperfections, your unmet goals, and your unattained dreams. And, with these proven tools activated, you will experience a deep feeling of satisfaction, which is quite likely what you've been looking for all along. What's more, with this new peace of mind as your foundation, you will have more creativity and inspiration for all of your awesome dreams and goals, and you will get to *be* enough while you attain them.

I invite you to join the tribe of peaceful warriors who refuse to sell their souls for some unattainable mirage. So light a fire, grab a cozy blanket and pen—you're gonna want to mark up this book—and take this time just for you. It will be the greatest gift you can give yourself. If you're anything like my thousands of clients, you'll be so glad you did! Oh, and despite the numerous references to women, this book is applicable to everyone.

Chapter 1

We Teach What We Need to Learn

When I was growing up, a common buzz phrase was: "One day your ship will come in." One day . . . at a future and unknowable date . . . if you do everything right and then wait long enough . . . you'll get what you were hoping for. *Then* you will be happy, then you will be stable, then life will be predictable, then . . .

It was a familiar message that I never questioned, *until I did*.

From a very early age, I was always examining myself and others. I enjoyed observing human patterns and behaviors, and if a classmate was in some kind of trouble, I couldn't focus on schoolwork until I at least tried to fix the problem. If problems arose between friends, I stepped in—mediating before I knew what the word meant. It seemed a career in counseling was written in the stars. However, after failing at my first job as a counselor, I stumbled and doubted my life direction.

That counseling job was at a children's home in Asheville, North Carolina. The counselors were amazing, and the kids were fortunate to have such love and support. I went home each night with the children's stories weighing heavy on my soul. I heard stories of abuse and neglect, of loneliness and longing. To my utter dismay, I had to admit I was not cut out for the job. I wanted to *fix* these kids, to take away their pain, and I found myself exhausted and discouraged.

So I gave my notice. I felt like a failure—not just to those kids, but also to myself. I had spent four-plus years studying social work and psychology, graduating with a counseling degree, and yet I didn't last a month in that field. What was I going to do?

I decided to go back to what I knew: waitressing. It paid the bills and

I was damn good at it. Still in Asheville, I got a job at the Biltmore Estate where I served generous tourists, and the tips rocked.

Yet while my pockets were full, my heart was empty. My true calling seemed a million miles away. I felt I had gifts that I wasn't using. I did, however, have a deep connection with God and the Universe, so after some late-night talks with God and lots of nature walks, I was reminded of a gift I might start tapping into.

While attending Warren Wilson College a few years earlier, I—with some discomfort—discovered that I was an "empath." An empath is one who has the ability to feel others' feelings. I clearly remember the day I was hanging out with my friend Josie and my ear started hurting. I looked at her and asked if she had an earache. This seemed to freak her out. She looked at me with a distorted face and said, "Yes! How did you know that?"

"Because my ear hurts," I said, "but I know there's nothing wrong with it." I winced slightly as I confessed this, from the familiar combination of feeling embarrassed yet affirmed.

Josie said she thought I was weird, and I think she scooted a little farther away on the cafeteria bench.

While this episode didn't help our friendship, it did help me own this gift, despite the potential separation I felt from those who didn't get me. The experience of feeling other people's feelings was not new, but I had done a good job of hiding it. I had always been sensitive to others' thoughts and feelings. Now, with trepidation, I was ready to begin owning it.

The amazing thing was, I didn't even know that I *hadn't* been owning it. The truth was I had shoved this gift to the side because it made me feel so different, and I had allowed the pain of separation to snuff out my light. My desperate desire to be accepted was now being challenged by my even more desperate desire to be me.

So, there I was. A college grad feeling like a counseling failure, knowing I didn't want to waitress the rest of my life, and an empath who couldn't even help herself.

It was time for some serious introspection.

My grandmother's best friend lived in Santa Barbara, California, and she invited me to come visit. The summer was approaching, so I gathered my waitressing loot and bought a ticket to the West Coast. Upon arriving I found my trusty waitress job (oh, dear God); but I also found a whole different vibe! Santa Barbara was a great town with positive energy. I quickly met interesting people who spoke of the mind-body connection, and I felt as though they were speaking *my* language. A language that had been foreign until then. After an insightful California summer, with answers to some heady questions, I returned to North Carolina and enrolled in a bunch of classes on the body-mind connection. I felt I was making some progress.

Then I met Dr. Rick Moss, who had started the Center for Pre-Cognitive Re-Education in Carmel, California. He'd come to North Carolina to visit his father, and he offered "Pre-Cog" sessions while in town. Pre-cognitive re-education helps people identify the subconscious, limiting beliefs that block them from what they really want to create, and gives them tools to turn those limiting beliefs into conscious, affirming ones.

We Are Not Our Beliefs

After one session with Rick, I knew I wanted to learn more. In that session, I saw the younger aspect of me—little Liz—who never felt enough. The "never enough" feeling was so familiar. Around friends I wasn't funny enough; around guys, never pretty enough; in school, never smart enough. Even when I gave someone a birthday present, I cringed inside and wondered, "Did I give enough?"

It's almost funny now, but the way we torture ourselves isn't funny at all. It's debilitating and destructive, and feels palpable as I write this. But it's something we can—*must*—stop, which is why I wrote this book.

In the session with Dr. Moss, I saw my life flash before my eyes, including all the decisions I had made based on that "never enough" belief system—the jobs I chose, the relationships I attracted, and the limitations I placed on my visions of the future.

But then the magic happened: I realized that when I separated myself from these *beliefs*, and saw that I still existed—I could see clearly that I was NOT those limiting beliefs. One by one I separated myself from each belief, almost like a cartoon character with a thought bubble above her head—remove the thought bubble (the limiting belief), and the character is still there.

This was a real revelation for me. I knew those old limiting beliefs came from many different places—messages I'd heard over the years; fears I'd held on to; things people said to me, like when Josie called me weird and scooted away from me in the school cafeteria.

But now that I could separate out those limiting beliefs, I gained access to the *real* me. The me I had been so good at hiding and shoving to the side and worrying about. This kind of work felt so familiar to my soul, I knew I wanted to learn more and use it to help others.

Would the "not pretty, smart, or good enough" thoughts reappear? Oh, yes! But with the understanding that we live in a society that breeds continual "not enough" beliefs and reinforces them with constant comparisons, I knew I had the tools to get past those thoughts. I knew I didn't have to live or act that way anymore. I could separate out from the limiting belief character and *be* enough.

This new awareness that we are NOT our limiting beliefs empowered me to write my new story—and to help others do the same.

When we're aware of what we're telling ourselves—when we unmask our insecurities and align with who we *really* are—we can shine. In fact, we can't stop ourselves from shining. When we separate ourselves from those crippling images that hold us back, they begin to vanish like the mirages they are. We get glimpses of heaven on earth.

We no longer have to wait for "one day," because we see that our ship has been there all along.

Helping Others Climb on Board

What does it take to make this shift? Turns out, some days it's easier than others. After the momentous realization that my thoughts and I were *not* one and the same, and years of intensive study on the subject, I began teaching workshops across the country. I was passionate about helping others learn how to separate themselves from their stories, to identify less with past hurts, and to live in the powerful present.

I continued to study with several teachers, including Patricia Crane and Rick Nichols in the *Heal Your Life* program, which is based on the philosophy of the beloved Louise Hay. *Heal Your Life* reinforces the power that positive affirmations have on one's life. I am honored to be certified in this teaching, as I believe that everything I teach I also need to learn. The teacher must always take the seat of the student.

Most recently, my student seat took the form of becoming a certified teacher and success coach in the *Canfield Success Principles*—another great training that feels familiar to my soul. These principles teach the necessity of putting yourself in the driver's seat, taking responsibility for your life, thinking positively, and remembering that your past does not dictate your future.

I created my own coaching company and called it *Pinnacle View*— because a shift in perception *will* put you on top of the world. For more than two decades I have coached hundreds of clients and inspired audiences around the globe with these principles.

I am grateful for the work I get to do each day, the reminders that I still need to practice, and the tribe of friends who support me.

I do know that *my ship has already come in*, and having the audacity to choose such a concept sends me on the ride of my life: a ride that creates a huge paradigm shift—from the ever-hopeful, unattainable *future* to the delicious, manifesting *present*! I jumped on board—with all my perfect imperfections, all my unreached goals, all my unattained wealth, and all my insecurities that (yes) still follow me around.

These days I feel liberated, and I experience a lightness in my step that was not there back when I was under the debilitating spell of focusing on who I was not, what I had not attained, and how I feared the future. I'm here to help you feel lighter, too.

Enough Already!

What I bring you in this book is offered as a gift—the gift of helping you see who you really are. In these pages, I will assist you in letting go of limiting beliefs, past wounds, and feelings of not being enough that may be holding you back. I will hand you the mirror and allow you to see the amazing you—who has been there all along.

With this gift you will gain tools to help you design your life with more hope, enhanced joy, greater awareness, and deeper satisfaction. You will experience deeper trust in your inner wisdom and intuition, and a stronger connection with Spirit. It is a whole new journey. And one, I find, that we have all been searching for.

This book is filled with lessons that have transformed my own ever-evolving life and the lives of my clients and audiences. I am living proof that we teach what we need to learn, and I am eager to help you discover—open your eyes to—the magic of who you already are *today*!

Now is the time; here is the place.

You have already arrived. Yes, you are *enough already*!

Home

We are on a journey home.
Home to ourselves.
It's a journey of discarding old stories and claiming the new.
It's one that will surely have you arrive . . . right where you've always dreamed you could be.
Right where you already are. Enough!

—Elizabeth Trinkaus

Labyrinth creation by Jennifer L. Potts

Chapter 2

Doubting Dotty and Believing Betty

A couple of characters weaseled their way into my book. Allow me to introduce you to Doubting Dotty and Believing Betty. Perhaps you will recognize them.

Doubting Dotty believes:

- her "happy" is somewhere out there
- she is never quite good enough
- she will be happy when she loses __ pounds, has __ partner, and makes $ __
- nearly everyone else has it better
- she is somehow flawed

Believing Betty believes:

- that joy and satisfaction in life are in this present moment
- her best is enough
- she is a miracle . . . (and so are you)
- she can shift from the inner critic to compassion
- that despite the goals she has yet to achieve, she has already arrived, and she is already enough

Doubting Dotty is likely very familiar—to you, and your preceding generations! The messages are subtle, yet incessant. They present a life-sucking energy that you want to make go away, but can't. Without the proper tools, it's like trying to push a buoy under water. Guess what—it pops back up again.

Believing Betty, on the other hand, understands that no one is a stranger to the doubter within; Betty knows with certainty that you have choices. You have the choice to shift your thinking, every minute of every day. With lots of proven tools, you can make the shifts you need to make. You can see you are . . . already enough.

Your Turn...

Each of us has thoughts like those of Believing Betty and Doubting Dotty. In order for you to get clear about what yours might be, take time to write down a few examples that seem familiar to you.

I feel like Doubting Dotty when I think:

I feel like Believing Betty when I think:

Two Birds

Two birds circle above me.
One flapping its wings frantically.
One soaring effortlessly.
I know how they both feel.
I'm drawn to the effortless glide.
I am reminded . . . to be like water.

—Elizabeth Trinkaus

I'm Afraid I Am That Kind of Girl

The experiences you have every day, that affect every corner of your life, depend entirely on *whom* you listen to. Imagine you're tuned in to the radio. Which station is preset for you? If you're being bombarded with negative chatter, like a snarky "shock jock" constantly railing against you, are you willing to switch stations? Will you do it—now?

I'm Afraid I Am That Kind of Girl Who:

Worries what others think
Believes she has to do more to feel enough
Looks in the mirror and sees the flaws
Gets insecure before she speaks
Doesn't know how to stop
Feels guilty when she says "no"
Judges herself
That girl who is tired . . .

I stand before you now . . . because I was that kind of girl, and one day I refused to be. With the help of great teachers and daily reminders . . .

I Am the Kind of Girl Who:

Worries less what others think
Reminds herself her best is enough
Looks in the mirror and has learned to say, "I love you"
Dances with discomfort and speaks her truth
Has learned to slow down
Notices the guilt wave and sends it out to sea
Judges herself, then chooses to love
Opens a door, takes a deep breath, and says, "I've got this."

Your Turn . . .

Are you willing to look at some of the things you tell yourself on a regular basis? Are you open to shifting what is no longer serving you? Have fun with it. Play with these possibilities . . .

Fill in your own poems here.

I'm Afraid I Am the Kind of Girl Who:

I Am the Kind of Girl Who:

Chapter 3

Statistically Speaking, You Really Are a Miracle

When my GPS says, "You've arrived at your destination," I take in a deep breath and let go. Ahhh, I have arrived . . . at my desired destination.

What if I lived my life in this state—as though I have *already* arrived, that I am "enough" now—instead of believing that the good stuff is *j-u-s-t* around the corner, out there somewhere? How would I feel? How would I act? How would my life be different?

Let's explore the possibility of living as though we have already arrived—*every day*—and experience the audacity of such a choice.

Think about your own internal GPS. What is it set to find? What if you really are a miracle?

Consider the Statistics

We are here, breathing, in human form. Do you know the statistics for such a phenomenon? The chance of that happening at all? Get ready for this: Scientists proclaim that the probability of you being born is about one in 400 trillion! Stop and take that in for a moment.

One in 400 trillion! (Trust me for now. We'll explain the math below.)

When I first heard this statistic, I was astonished. It was a challenge to wrap my head around it. The sheer enormity of such a number had me pause, ride the fine line of belief and disbelief, and truly consider approaching my life differently. One in 400 trillion—this information put a spin on life that wasn't there before. It propelled a newfound appreciation of my own and everyone else's existence. A less-pressured calling began to tug at me, and I had new eyes with which to navigate this journey. Whoa! Perhaps I am a miracle . . .

...And so are you!

Dr. Ali Binazir details the math behind this phenomenon in his blog post "What Are the Chances of Your Coming into Being?"[1] He says he'd heard something similar in the Buddhist version, which imagines there is one life preserver thrown into an ocean, and one turtle swimming underwater somewhere. The probability that you exist today is the same as that turtle sticking its head out of the water and into the middle of that life preserver in just one try!

He follows his story by informing us that the total area of the world's oceans is 131.6 million square miles, the life preserver's hole is about 30 inches in diameter, and probability of the turtle sticking its head into that life preserver is about one in 700 trillion.

Binazir writes: "One in 400 trillion vs. one in 700 trillion are pretty darn close, for such a farfetched notion from two completely different sources: old-time Buddhist scholars and present-day scientists. They agree to within a factor of two!"

He then explains the probability of your parents meeting. If they met one new person of the opposite sex every day for 25 years, that would be almost 10,000 people. And the probability of your parents' meeting resulting in kids is about one in 2,000.

The probability is already around one in 40 million, and now we are about to deal with eggs and sperm! A fertile woman has about 100,000 viable eggs and a man will produce about 12 trillion sperm over the course of his lifetime. The probability of one sperm hitting that one egg is one in 400 quadrillion.

Add in the chances of your ancestors—all 150,000 generations!—reproducing successfully, and the chances of you being here rocket to 1 in 10 to the 2.65 millionth power. Or 1 followed by 2.5 million zeros.

Binazir offers yet another way of considering the probability of your existing. It's like the probability of two million people getting together

---

[1] See http://blogs.harvard.edu/abinazir/2011/06/15/what-are-chances-you-would-be-born. Accessed Feb. 2018. All references and quotations in this section have been taken from this source.

to play a game of dice—with *trillion-sided dice*. When each of those two million people rolls the dice, they all come up the exact same number!

Writes Benazir: "A miracle is an event so unlikely as to be almost impossible. By that definition, I've just shown that you are a miracle. Now go forth and feel and act like the miracle that you are."

Being open to the possibility of living your life as a miracle every day—as though you have already arrived, completely and entirely enough—is a powerful choice. It is healthy medicine for your evolution. And its benefits, well, they're like those really big numbers, like the ones you'd find on a pair of trillion-sided dice.

Every side is a miracle. And yes, you are too!

> *You weren't an accident. You weren't mass-produced. You aren't an assembly-line product. You were deliberately planned, specifically gifted, and lovingly positioned on the earth by the Master Craftsman.*
> —Max Lucado

You're Enough NOW

The statistics are a huge wake-up call, aren't they? For you to truly digest this, you have to be open to the possibility that you are a miracle *already*.

Now. Today.

Sit with that for a moment. What if this is true? I get that you make the choice to even *begin* to think this way. But what if you choose to? What might be the outcome?

This shift in mindset could give you the ability to examine every corner of your life, which in turn opens the door for a grand appreciation for the present moment and enhances your ability to bring profound joy to this most precious journey. Wowza!

Seeing yourself as a miracle puts a new spin on the old and very familiar belief:

I will be not be enough until I have . . .

that job,

or *that* partner,

or *that* money,

or *that* house,

or *that* weight.

All of these notions steal the very joy of today and zap that which you truly desire more than anything—to be happy NOW.

Separate your goals from your happy-source. Dreams and goals are so exciting and motivating, the trick is not handing over your "happy" to your perceived dream destination . . . out there *somewhere*. You know, that mirage you see shimmering on the highway in the distance (more on that in the next chapter).

Is it even possible to be in this present moment? To stop long enough to begin noticing what you are telling yourself, and actually draw on all the benefits of owning the miracle that you are? What would happen if you did? What a mind-blowing concept! Let's find out!

What if your journey is priceless? What if you are so incredibly lucky to be here and you are already enough today? Of course, there are improvements to make and goals to achieve, but imagine that today, at this very sacred moment, you are supposed to be here. Right where you are now.

Take it in.

That state of realizing *I am already enough* has the potential to create a foundation of inspiration, peppered with grace. A whispering into your ear: "I am farther along than I thought. Maybe I *do* have this!" It can be the crack that lets in a sliver of light. And that sliver is enough to light the way.

This feeling of ease, or grace, spreads the potential for a deeper satisfaction that was somehow missing when you were so busy living in the inaccessible future, a place that is truly impossible to inhabit. Living in this new state of now-ness is not only doable, it has the capacity to create paradigm shifts that will illuminate multiple aspects of your life—not to mention the ripple effects—in ways that will surely delight you.

It wasn't until I learned to push aside our culture's incessant habit of comparing, which creates huge fears and insecurities, that I could have moments of experiencing the peace that comes with feeling, having, and being "enough." I realized I was enough, and I'm honored to assist in holding that understanding for others.

When I host retreats, we do an exercise in which everyone is given the opportunity to separate themselves from all the "stuff" they're used to carrying around (we're talking mental stuff here). Because most of us are so aligned with our mental stuff—past wounds, present worries, future fears—it can be enormously liberating to drop all that baggage and align with who we really are.

And I promise, from this inspired and more satisfied state, you can learn to be kinder to yourself and others, and you will naturally achieve your goals more quickly. Your breaths will become deeper and your innate inclination to trust the journey will become more prominent. Your intuition will speak with a louder voice, and accessing your wisdom will become second nature.

Chapter 4

86 the Mirage

You see the mirage: It seems so real, the glimmer of water on the dry highway in front of you. With anticipation, you get closer, then . . . it disappears. It happens again, then again.

Perhaps *next* time it will be there. Perhaps *next* time you will arrive. This familiar message may play out in your life. The idea that success is just around the corner—until you get there and realize it must be around the next corner, until you get there and realize it must be around the next one . . .

This process is like viewing a mirage, watching it get closer and closer and then fade into nothingness. With this thought process, how are we ever going to be enough? How can we ever fully arrive?

Many of us feel this way. We think if we could just afford a house in this neighborhood or that gated community; if we get the right salary, the right partner, the right granite countertop, the right children . . . *then* we will have arrived. Then we'll be able to kick back and bask in our contentment.

Except we never do. (Or if we do, it's not for long.)

Let's be clear that the right salary, partner, and house are wonderful. But full satisfaction can come only if we know that we are *enough already*—from the inside out—even though there are things we will always be working toward.

The new awareness of this "inside job" has empowered many of my clients to create successful life designs. They've gone from waiting for enjoyment to realizing they can enjoy the day right now. This frees them up to be authentic, to focus on what's real and what's possible, and in many cases it has led them to make better decisions about their careers and sounder choices in their relationships. It all starts with knowing that they are enough already.

Back in my waitressing days, we used the number "86" as a term to mean we were out of something—salmon, chicken—and we needed to erase it from our mental menu. Or we'd ask the maître d' to "86 the person at the end of the bar" if they were getting unruly and needed to be sent packing.

Let's do the same to the seductive but unruly trickster—the mirage. If your enough-ness was "out there" somewhere, you would have found it by now.

The Real Reason I Failed

Remember that first job I got after studying to become a counselor? I was in Asheville, North Carolina, working with abused and neglected kids in a children's home. I went to bed at night exhausted, because try as I might—and I did—I just couldn't fix those kids. I couldn't get them turned around and back on track.

I know now why I failed at that job: because I was trying to fix the children, rather than seeing that they were already enough. By focusing on what I felt they were missing, I missed seeing—more importantly, missed helping them to see—all their strengths and gifts and perfect imperfections that together made them the miracles that they truly were. Then, now, and always. No one could change the neglectful circumstances those kids had come from; but they needed me to show them they were miracles *despite* this—miracles in their own right.

It was a missed opportunity on my end, but I hope and believe I have made up for lost time and learned from my failures.

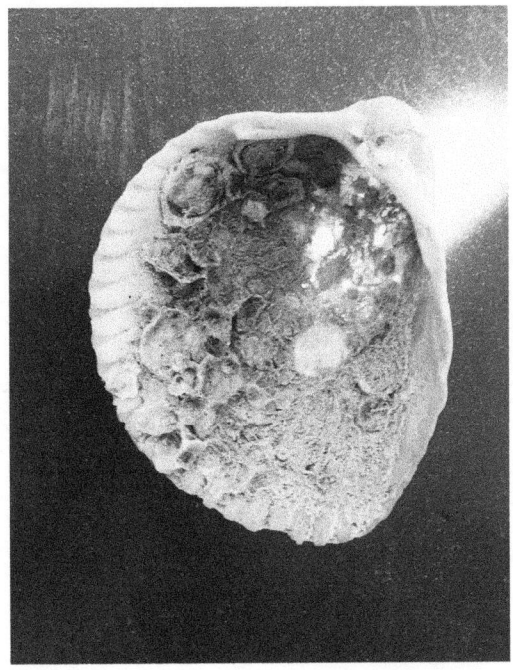

There is a crack in everything; that's how the light gets in.
—Leonard Cohen

Your Turn ...

1. Take a moment and fill in the blanks. You may be surprised at some of your answers. Keep writing until you run out of space.

    I will be happy when:

I will be happy if:

2. Stop. Notice how this future thinking has the potential to rob you of your joy in this moment. Goals are necessary, but don't confuse them with your ability to be content in the present.

   What if you are enough already? How would that make you feel?

   What might be holding you back, or preventing you from feeling this way?

   What if you could "86" the belief(s) holding you back? Then how might you feel?

Chapter 5

Our Thoughts Affect Everything

Dr. Masaru Emoto was a Japanese researcher who was passionate about the power of thoughts. I appreciate his numerous studies, and hope they'll live on for generations.[2]

Dr. Emoto spent years proving that human consciousness can change the molecular structure of water. He proved that water physically responds to our negative and positive thoughts and words, and that polluted water could be cleansed through positive thoughts and visualizations. He proved this by photographing the effects of thoughts on water crystals, and determined that the positive ones created orderly crystal formations, while the negative ones created chaotic formations.

Our human bodies are somewhere between 60 percent (adults) to 75 percent (babies) water. Imagine how our thoughts affect the water within us, and how that impacts our lives each day.

Dr. Emoto's findings have made me more aware of what I am telling myself. They've provided a great tool in nudging me to shift from thinking negative to thinking positive thoughts, from being critical to being more compassionate, and from focusing on feelings of lack to focusing on those of abundance.

At the opening ceremony of my retreats, I speak about Dr. Emoto's studies and give each participant a water bottle. I instruct them to come up with an intention, one that they will literally "drink in" all weekend. Examples include: I am a powerful force for good. I am shining. I trust my journey. I am enough.

My favorite experiment of Dr. Emoto's is the power of thoughts on

---

[2] Check out Dr. Emoto's *New York Times* best seller, *The Hidden Messages in Water*, and more of his work online at http://www.masaru-emoto.net.

jars of cooked rice. He took two jars of rice, labeled one LOVE and the other HATE, and instructed schoolchildren to think about the jars each day as they entered their class. He asked them to send loving thoughts to the LOVE jar and hateful thoughts to the HATE jar.

What do you imagine happened? After thirty days, the LOVE jar of cooked rice remained the same, while the HATE jar of cooked rice had rotted!

In his teachings, Dr. Emoto encourages all of us to try these experiments—and most importantly, to be aware of the thoughts we are telling ourselves. Our thoughts can be healthy medicine or destructive poison. We all have negative thoughts. The power comes from paying attention, and then making the choice to shift from destructive, negative thoughts to powerful, positive ones.

While some skeptics debunk Dr. Emoto's work and insist his findings could be mere coincidence, his petri dishes contaminated, etc., I choose to live confidently with the knowledge that our thoughts do have profound effects on our lives.

I had the opportunity to experience this when I was 13 and my parents came home with a surprise—an abandoned female dog that was full of mange. She seemed emotionally scarred by the world, had open wounds, and no hair.

The vet told us there was no hope for her, and we probably should just put her down. We left the vet's office with this dog in the backseat, wrapped up in a blanket.

One neighbor suggested we name her Mangey. Mom had a different idea. She named her *Beautiful*. Every day we called her B-e-a-u-t-i-f-u-l. Within three weeks her hair started to grow back and her wounds began to heal. Within eight weeks she had a full, new coat and a notable new trust in her disposition. Beautiful thrived, and that experience opened my eyes even wider to the power of our thoughts and the possibilities of miracles.

Experiencing firsthand healings and watching lives become transformed with positive thoughts and prayers have made me a believer, teacher, and preacher. Thanks, Dr. Emoto.

Your Turn . . .

Imagine YOU are a glass of water (which, in a way, you are), and that everything you think and say will have a profound effect on you.

What thoughts and words will you send your own way?

Chapter 6

Switching the Station

We all have favorite songs that inspire us and make us want to burst out singing. And then there are those songs that, for whatever reason, we never want to hear again (Phil Collins's "In the Air Tonight"... *sorry, Phil!*). When they come on, we change the station. Boom, done. On to the next tune.

Now ask yourself these questions: Do I have the ability to switch the station *in my head*? The power to switch from victim to victor? From the inner critic to the voice of compassion? To release the nagging, energy-sucking, bitter friend and hang with the motivating bestie?

The answers are *yes*. What happens next is the shifting of a huge pattern. And when you make this shift, you open yourself to the fabulous floodgates of feeling your power. You're in the driver's seat, taking yourself on a journey that will lead you to greater peace and brighter outcomes, that will likely end in a happy dance.

Remember, you already hold the most powerful tool in the Universe—the power to shift your thinking.

Every thought holds a vibration, and that vibration either gives us energy or depletes our energy. We are said to have about 60,000 thoughts a day. Of these, 95 percent (57,000) are repeats, and 80 percent (48,000) are "negative."[3] While we can certainly work on changing that boatload of negative thoughts to positive ones, we can also try to move out of our thought ruts and infuse our thinking with what's fresh and new!

Perhaps you remember the billboards and commercials in which

---

[3] This statistic is often attributed to the National Science Foundation. Some scientists estimate we could have as many as 100,000 thoughts in a day!

Smokey Bear, in his official forest ranger hat and his sincere but serious voice, told us, "Only YOU can prevent forest fires."[4]

Let's recast Smokey's message as a reminder to keep our negative thoughts from burning holes in our best lives: "Only YOU have the power to change the way you think."

To put this another way—and there's nothing wrong with playing around with images until we find one that sticks for us—let's go back to the metaphor of the radio. The one in the car when you're by yourself and on comes that song you NEVER want to hear again. Remember: "Only YOU have the power to change the station."

"But, Elizabeth," you say, "changing the stations on a car radio is one thing. How do I change the negative chatter yammering away in my head?"

"One step at a time," I reply. "One step at a time."

Steps to Help You Switch the Station in Your Head

Step 1: Be willing to stop . . . and listen.

Yes, really listen to the jumble of junk so you can get ready to take it down, piece by piece. This takes discipline and courage.

---

[4] In 2001 the campaign slogan was changed to: "Only YOU can prevent wildfires."

Step 2: Be willing to look.

Oftentimes the negative stories were created in childhood. Understand that we are not blaming our past. The blaming of our past only keeps us in a victim state. To be victorious, allow yourself to be in the powerful present and remind yourself that you have the power to shift patterns.

Step 3: Notice when you're ready to throw in the towel.

Perhaps you feel that you're failing not just this week, but you've been a failure all along, and (the crummy station says) you will NEVER be enough. Remember this: Just because you hear it doesn't make it true. (This is especially easy to envision, given our "post-truth" society and the prevalence of "fake news.") Some of your self-chatter is like that fake news! Never was true, and never will be true.

Now's the time to SWITCH stations to the one blasting the message: "My best is enough." You might not feel this way right now, but stay on this station anyway. You'll get it soon enough.

Step 4: Ask yourself, "What encouraging words would I tell a friend if she was the one struggling?"

You might say, "You've overcome much worse," or "You've totally got this."

Hint: If you say these affirmations out loud, they become a positive-vibration radio station for you!

Step 5: Hold the energy of that best-friend message, the positive-vibration radio station.

Compassion, love . . . breathe it in . . . If it's true for her, it's true for you, too.

Step 6: Live as though you're enough already. Because you *are*.

Fill your tool kit with reminders and create a tribe of positive people you feel good around.

As we move forward, I'd like you to do what I call "SNL." No, I'm not talking about the very funny TV show *Saturday Night Live*, but Stop, Notice, Love. If you find yourself stuck in an infinite loop of negative self-chatter, and for some reason you can't switch stations, then SNL. STOP what you're doing; NOTICE what you're thinking; and LOVE yourself anyway.

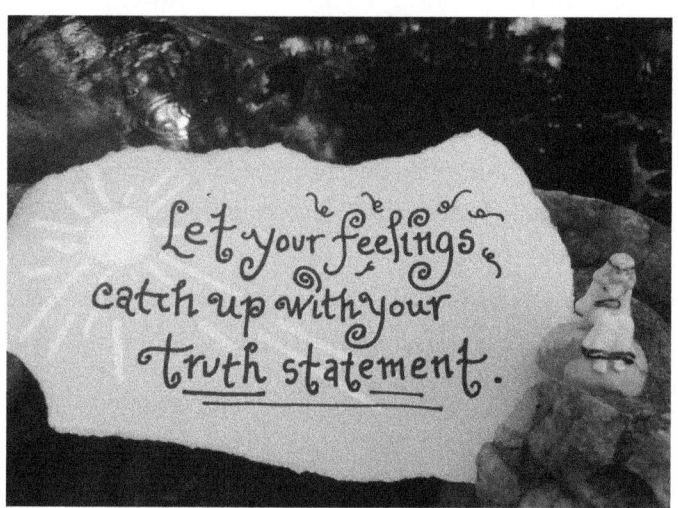

Breaking Free

When we make the conscious effort to choose self-compassion
over the cruel critic,
live in the present instead of the regrets of the past,
embrace the miracle we are today,
we have broken the spell that kept us doubting.
Breaking free!
We now have license to own our gifts,
do great work in the world,
and love the life we've been given.

—Elizabeth Trinkaus

Your Turn . . .

Use this quick tool to raise your vibe.

Every thought holds a vibration. How might we vibrate higher throughout each day in order to feel better? Here's a quick tool to assist you in raising your vibrational level.

Grab your pen and make a list of 10 things you've accomplished in your life. But before you get started, take a deep breath, let go of the idea that they all must be lofty accomplishments, exhale, and—most importantly—enjoy the process.

10 Accomplishments in My Life

1.

2.

3.

4.

5.

6.

7.

8.

9.

10.

Now read your list. Pretty cool, huh? Sit in that positive, high vibration. It is likely different from the one you are so accustomed to dwelling on if you're used to focusing on what you *didn't do*.

This one is rich in character, creativity, and the juiciness of life! Take it in. Take it with you! Practice sitting in this good-feeling vibration for five minutes every day. What will happen? You will experience more energy, creativity, inspiration, and joy. This is your natural state, and it's patiently waiting for you to align with it.

If you had fun with these 10 accomplishments, try another 10—or 5, or 12—next week. And again, sit high in the joy of achievement, big and small.

And remember to be grateful for the opportunities that arose in order for you to achieve these items on your list.

Just Stop It!

Have you ever looked back at photos and thought, "Oh. My. God! I *was* really pretty, thin, cute, happy, or _____ back then! But I thought I was ugly, fat, sad, or_____!"?

Too often we think we're not enough, but when we're given the opportunity to look back on ourselves, we realize we were! We failed to appreciate how amazing we were in that present moment. On the other hand, we often look back and associate the past with positive memories—as if we don't recall how negatively we saw ourselves back then.

Sound familiar?

It was for me until I refused to live this energy-sucking model. Because that's what it does—sucks our energy by preying on our insecurities—like the dementors in J. K. Rowling's Harry Potter books. (She said the dementors were metaphors for depression, which she had experienced.)

By contrast, when I practice being vigilant, I remain conscious of what I am telling myself and choose the voice of compassion—even when the critic is screaming in my ears (and boy, can it scream!). Again, this is a matter of practice, not simply divine inspiration. Be conscious, choose compassion, and bring the power of amazing you—yes, YOU—to today. There is *only* today!

These *are* the good ole days!

Your Turn . . .

Grab your pen. You're going to like this one. *Believing Betty is smiling at us.*

1. My age is: _____. (For example, I am 40.)
2. Add 10 years and you are_____. (E.g., 50)
3. Imagine you are 10 years older (e.g., 50, from #2) and you have a mirror into *today*.
4. Make a list of what you appreciate about today/you/your life.
   1.
   2.
   3.
   4.
   5.

These are the good ole days that we've been livin'
No more lookin' back; all is forgivin'
Ain't gonna live my life through no picture frame
These are the good ole days.
—James Otto

Chapter 7

An Exercise Typically Reserved for the Dead

Last year I was having dinner with Greg, my life squeeze of more than two decades, when a woman approached our table and said to me, "You probably don't remember me, but 10 years ago you taught a workshop at UNC and you asked us to write our eulogy. It was the most incredible exercise I've ever done, and I still think about it today. To live from a place of *who I am*, instead of *who I am not* has changed my life."

I thanked her for having the courage to come over to our table and share her experience with me, and then I had to take a minute to soak it in.

I recall that workshop well. I had created a Carolina Women's Group that included a workshop for each event. Let me tell you, writing your own eulogy was not one of the most popular activities, as you can imagine. I was met with a wide range of emotions. Some shock, some disapproval, some "This is going to be fascinating!" All those who participated (yes, some didn't) were blown away by what they wrote!

Writing your own eulogy can be a mind-bending exercise that has you revealing your gifts today while allowing you to enter that blissful state of letting go of all the striving, limitations, and imperfections. You're going to focus on what you've achieved, and who you've become. You are *not* writing about what you *didn't* accomplish (though if you do, fire yourself and start over).

Some compare the effects of this exercise to the awesome laughing gas (nitrous oxide) you get when you go for a root canal (if you're lucky enough to have had one of those). You are in a state of chilling out, with the critic in your head silenced.

In fact, this mental state is accessible NOW, even without the drug—when you *choose* it. What a way to live!

Your Turn . . .

Here is your opportunity to write your eulogy. If you have some resistance, I suggest you do it anyway. It has proven to be an exercise that has the potential to create welcome shifts. Try it for yourself.

Eulogy for _____ (your name)

_____(your name) was _____.
S/he was a wonderful _____,
and s/he loved to _____.

(Get creative with all the descriptors you might include: best friend, mother, sailor, scientist, baker, nature lover, artist, teacher, lawyer, nurse, etc.)

Now write 10 to 20 more things for your eulogy. Breathe. Then read them through.

Well done!

I suggest you take time to reread your list often. It will help you remember your accomplishments and align with your essence. It will be a reminder that who you are is amazingly enough. Gratitude is sure to follow.

Don't Wait 'til You're Dead

Why is it when someone dies, we give ourselves license to open our hearts and express without filters all the great things we knew about this person? I remember when Michael Jackson died; I was struck by the worldwide magnitude of people who came out to pay homage. MJ was amazing. He was talented, and he was wounded. I only wish he had gotten—understood—who he really was, instead of who he was not. If he had, perhaps he would be alive today.

Last year we were sad to say good-bye to Greg's wonderful father, Jim. After he passed, we hosted a Celebration of Life gathering at our home in North Carolina. People traveled from all over the country, including a young couple from Mississippi. They came to pay their respects and to celebrate what Jim had meant to them. I will never forget the silence that blanketed the room as the woman told the story of how Jim had believed in her, hired her, and how her entire life was transformed because of him.

She said, "I never thought I'd have more than a minimum-wage job. But Jim believed in me and helped me to believe in myself. Now my husband and I are running the company! I have come here to thank Jim for changing my life."

We were all so moved by her story, and I wondered in that moment whether Jim actually realized what a difference he had made in her life. Was he aware of the way his caring, compassion, and belief in another person had truly transformed the life of this woman, her family, and no doubt others? I sure hope so.

But the sad truth is, most of us don't know. First, because we don't stop long enough to focus on the miracle that we are TODAY; and second, because most of us are too intimidated to open our hearts, look others in the eye, and express all the things we appreciate about them. Is it fear of rejection? Fear we might look or sound silly? Is it the discomfort that is coupled with vulnerability?

Take a moment and ask yourself.

Your Turn...

Here is your opportunity to make a list of some of the people who have really made a difference in your life. Why are you grateful to them? If they are still alive, are you willing to let them know?

Chapter 8

The Courage to Affirm

My friend JJ is the queen of opening her heart and expressing to others how she feels about them. She has inspired me to speak up more. If there are instances when I hesitate to call a friend who has lost a parent or pet, I stop and make the call anyway. I override needing to know what I'm going to say, other than "My heart breaks with you and I am here for you."

I'm always glad I made the call, and any previous self-conscious, vulnerable feelings become replaced with love. Perhaps it's ego—the fear of appearing foolish—that keeps us from reaching out to others in pain. Maybe we feel guilty that they are suffering and we are not. No matter what justifications we cobble together for ourselves to avoid it, acknowledging other people's pain and struggles lets them know we are holding them in our best and most compassionate thoughts. This brings connection instead of isolation.

Your Turn...

What are some things you have been wanting to do/say, but hold yourself back from doing/saying?

Whether the thought of pushing past this resistance is exciting or terrifying, I encourage you to get your energy moving and express yourself. And know you have made a difference.

"LIFE" – Buenos Aires, Argentina

The Healing Waters of the Affirmation Bath

At our retreats we do an exercise called the "Affirmation Bath." No, we don't get wet; but we do get bathed in light and positivity.

I first experienced an Affirmation Bath at a Louise Hay *Heal Your Life* training I took in Orlando, Florida, with the great Patricia Crane and Rick Nichols. After seven days of intensive work together, we, the participants, all *knew* each other. We had allowed ourselves to become vulnerable with each other, to show and let go of our supposed weaknesses, and to align with our true essence. Our teachers knew this was the time for our Affirmation Bath.

It's a simple exercise of being put into the "love seat"—not the "hot seat"—and then being surrounded by the group who are blurting out, unapologetically, in free-association style, all of our assets, strengths, and gifts.

"You're thoughtful! . . . You're beautiful! . . . You're so wise!"

You might think, *Wow, how cool is that!* Which it is. However, the fascinating part is, at first, it's strangely uncomfortable to align with these characteristics that *are* really who you are.

To hear the positive, loving statements over and over is mind altering. You pause and ask yourself, "Is that truly how I show up in the world? Could that be me? But I'm not always thoughtful. My hair doesn't look beautiful. Am I really . . . wise?"

But when you make the choice to take in these affirmations, you start feeling some positive side effects. You may be tempted to reject what you hear—"My hair may not look that bad, but did you see the bags under my eyes?"—but take in the positive anyway. Try it!

I did. And it felt good. No, it felt *great*.

No more excuses. Let's do this . . .

I highly encourage you to gather your "tribe" (even if that's just one friend) and experience an Affirmation Bath, or come to one of our Pinnacle View retreats and let us bathe you in your own brilliance!

Who Is She?

Similar to the eulogy-writing exercise, at our retreats we do a writing exercise called "Who Is She?" This also yields profound results, à la the Affirmation Bath, and allows people to achieve the *pinnacle view* that they so richly deserve. The exercise is simple. Just grab a pen and paper and start with the words "She is" (even though you're actually talking about yourself), and then let the rest follow. Sometimes writing or thinking in third person ("she" rather than "I") helps us see ourselves more generously.

Allow your mind to bend, your heart to open, that life of yours to be seen and felt—today!

Your Turn...

Write about the best gifts you bring to the world, and the girl inside who's not afraid to shine. Okay, maybe she is afraid to shine. Do it anyway. Don't allow the discomfort to rob you of this gift. If you need more pages, grab some notebook paper and keep writing!

Who is she?
　　　She is _____

Here's a portion of something a client wrote at my last retreat:

Who Is She?

She is kind, loving, and caring.
She is a fabulous leader.
She is beautiful and courageous.
She guides, nurtures, and supports other people whom she loves and cares about.
She speaks her truth and is trustworthy.
She is highly motivated and learning to own her worth.

Through my work, I have the privilege of helping people see, own, and absolutely live into who they are. In order to do that, sometimes we need to shift the old familiar stories people told us about being "too big for our britches," or the cruel comments like, "Who does she think she is?!" So many of us have been taught that shining—that is, speaking up and showing up—is egotistical, and that we are bragging about ourselves, overstepping our bounds, and perhaps thinking too highly of ourselves.

But there is a difference between hollow egotism and innate worth. What I'm talking about here is our essence as human beings, which often clashes with old messages we've received about who we were. Keep an eagle eye on what you're telling yourself, and don't allow those old messages to prevent you from shining and being the real you!

If you're up to this challenge, I encourage you to own your gifts, love who you are, and shine brightly . . . a little more each day.

The love you give to yourself is key to the love you give to others.
—Elizabeth Trinkaus

Chapter 9

N-O-W

Eckhart Tolle gave us the gift of remembering to slow down enough to enjoy this life journey a bit more. He is best known as the author of *The Power of Now* and *A New Earth: Awakening to Your Life's Purpose*.

Learning these lessons came at quite a cost to Tolle. He grew up in post-WWII Germany and absorbed the heavy energy around him. He became depressed and even suicidal. His turning point was a spiritual epiphany, when he had a deep shift in his thinking and separated out from the "I" (or self) and experienced the profound present moment. He called this peaceful presence "beingness." This inspired the writing of his first book, *The Power of Now*, in 1997, which reached the *New York Times* bestseller list in 2000.

What I admire about Tolle is the way he takes the simple context of NOW and gives us the opportunity to create notable shifts in our everyday experiences. For me it becomes a reminder to:

- **N = Notice**—to bring my focus to this very moment, not regrets from the past or fears of the future.
- **O = Observe**—to observe my thoughts, perhaps quiet the critic and embrace the encourager.
- **W = Win**—to embrace the feeling of winning. We can only win in the NOW. Not yesterday, not tomorrow, but now.

When you live in the NOW, you have, in a sense, set yourself free from the spell of the unknown, which always seems to conjure up very creative fears. The NOW. How simple. How powerful. It's another way to experience the reality that you have *already arrived*. That you are *enough already*! Enjoy it now, because *now* is all that there is.

(When I wrote this—in my head—I was standing in my driveway. I stopped. I brought all my focus to the present, the now. I observed. The birds chirping in the woods all of a sudden became so loud. What I knew was they were always that loud; I had just drowned them out with thoughts of what I had to do today, when company would arrive, what I needed to do to prepare, etc., etc. I noticed. I observed. I won.)

This practice in the midst of a busy day is a gift I give myself. And so can you. It doesn't take long and its effect is great medicine.

Practice it now. Bring your focus to this present moment. Observe. Win. Remember:

N = **Notice** this very moment.
O = **Observe** your thoughts; quiet the critic; embrace the encourager.
W = **Win** and embrace the feeling of victory.

Create space between the doing so that the miracles can enter!

Your Turn . . .

Own your gifts now.
1. Breathe.
2. Bring your energy to your feet. This gets you out of your head . . . and more hopeful. This is where *Believing Betty* begins to kick in.
3. Sit with your gift(s). Say them out loud. I *am* a good _____ (singer, guitar player, mom, listener, dancer, presenter, coach, cook, teacher, friend, etc.).
4. Be in the discomfort of it. If you don't sit with it, and feel it, you won't be able to OWN it.
5. Compare less. This doesn't mean you won't ever compare yourself to someone else. But it *does* mean you'll notice *when* you are doing this, and then you'll shift to compassion for yourself. Again, and again . . .
6. Be YOU (not that other singer, dancer, mom, coach).
7. Be rejected and judged. (Ouch, I know. Guess what, it has nothing to do with you. Releasing the fear of/resistance to *being* judged makes room for more courage. I promise.)
8. Do it anyway.
9. Laugh at your mistakes.
10. Find a tribe of powerful, supportive women.
11. Own your gift(s). The world needs you, and them . . .

Before a keynote speech or retreat, the tool that helps me most is releasing my resistance to fear. I've learned to accept—even to *expect*—the fear. When I let go of the "resistance" to fear, I free up my energy to have more fun. Even though I know this, I have to remind myself each time.

Chapter 10

My (Half) Marathon Story

Years ago, my friends Lisa and Mary were discussing the possibility of flying to Phoenix, Arizona, to run a half marathon. They were all in, meaning they knew they could do it, and they wanted me to join. They believed I could to it too, but I was paralyzed by fear and self-doubt. They assumed I was open to the possibility, but my self-doubt was so extreme that I had completely written off the possibility of trying.

Nonetheless, we were to meet for dinner on Tuesday to discuss the details. But I didn't even show up. I can't remember if I called to say I wasn't coming (and wasn't running), or if I just plain didn't show up. For the next 48 hours, my mind was obsessed with the idea, the question, "What if I *could* run this race?" That thought was quickly smothered by waves of fear through my body, and I expected the suggestion that I could actually do it would soon fade.

But it didn't fade. It rose again and again and would not leave me alone. Damn it!

When I expressed my doubts to Lisa, an avid runner, she said, "Sure you can do it!" Yet while I *trusted* her, I didn't *believe* her. I, the daily walker and occasional short-distance runner, was almost annoyed at the suggestion that I could actually run the race. Days passed, but the possibility did not.

I finally asked Greg what he thought, hoping he'd say, "Well, 13.1 miles *is* kinda far," and relieve me of my misery. His response was, "You'll never know if you don't try."

My reaction: *Oh sh*t! Seriously?* But I knew he was right.

By then it was November and I had eight weeks to go—from a girl who ran, at most, 3 miles, to a girl who was going to join 10,000 people and attempt 13.1 miles. It was time to get going, and I already felt *w-a-y* behind.

I began some serious self-talk conversations and reminded myself I didn't have to "run" the whole 13.1 miles. I could walk, I could crawl, I could even get picked up by that generous marathon worker who drives runners to the finish line long after the race has ended. I had choices. I had a goal.

I signed on the dotted line.

December arrived and I was increasing my miles, meaning from three miles to six. We would soon ring in the New Year, which meant in just weeks we would be boarding the plane.

I met my friends at the airport. I was excited, I was scared, and I had a seemingly endless list of questions for our five-hour flight. And the adventures had just begun. I asked, "What do you do if you have to go to the bathroom during the race?" and many other assorted questions. My friends laughed with me and filled me with answers.

Then the strangest thing happened. I looked up and noticed a woman getting up from her seat about five rows ahead. It was like that experience I mentioned earlier, when my college friend Josie had an earache. I could feel panic and it *wasn't* because of the upcoming race; it wasn't even mine. I got up immediately and Lisa and Mary asked where I was going.

"This woman is about to have a panic attack," I said. But simultaneously I thought to myself, "What *am* I doing?"

Despite the question in my head, however, I did not hesitate. I met the distraught woman in the aisle and told her it was going to be okay. At this point, the flight attendants knew something was wrong and made room for us at the back of the plane. We sat. The woman was clearly shaken and was crying a lot. I stayed with her and held her hand.

The flight attendants peeked in every now and then, but made themselves pretty scarce. Meanwhile, the woman's tears fell and we took deep breaths together. She assured *me* she would be okay, and I reminded her to take her time. After several minutes, which seemed like an hour, her breathing slowed down and she relaxed. She said she just found out her husband, a preacher, was having an affair with her neighbor. Oh. My. God. I just held the space for her and we breathed some more. She thanked me, said she was meeting a good friend in Phoenix, and knew she was going to be okay.

I joined my girlfriends and took some time to process what had unfolded. A couple of flight attendants came up and thanked me, which was very thoughtful.

We soon landed, checked into our hotel, and carbed up at a yummy restaurant. The next day we got up, and it was GAME time! We grabbed our lattes and I knew there was no turning back. All I had was my trusty water bottle, positive affirmations to recite, and many fears of the unknown that I attempted to tame.

Before I knew it I found myself at the starting line. There I was, standing with *real* runners. My heart was racing with excitement, and I tried to allow the fear to flow through me, knowing that resisting it would use up my much-needed energy. I continued to recite positive affirmations, take many deep breaths, and remind myself that I could stop whenever I needed to. The most important thing was: I showed up!

Then came the countdown: "5 – 4 – 3 – 2 – 1!" A gun fired, and tens of thousands of people I had *just* been stretching with were now mere *dots* in front of me. "Can I really do this?" I asked myself. "Just keep going," another voice said. And so I ran, I breathed, and I tracked each conversation in my head—knowing that one could cause huge anxiety and the other, well, potential victory.

It was a Rock & Roll Marathon, which meant every mile there was a new band playing. I ran. And I ran. I remember vividly seeing the large MILE 7 sign ahead of me. I was blown away. I had never run seven miles. I didn't even know it was possible. I was OVER halfway there!!

I asked myself, "What if I could do eight? . . . nine?"

By then there were hundreds of people lining the streets cheering us all on, saying things like "You can do it!" and "Go, go, go!" Tears were streaming down my face. I took in every word and kept running. I passed mile eight, then nine.

And then my eyes locked onto . . . MILE 10. OMG! What if I can run 11?

I rounded another corner and there was 11. The cheering got louder and my tears kept flowing. Could I do two more? My thighs were barking big-time, but I assured them that a hot tub was in their near future and the pain was temporary. I kept going, in disbelief. And then, there was MILE 12. Then . . . the finish line!!!

By that point I was having an out-of-body experience, observing something I didn't know was truly possible.

I crossed the finish line and a volunteer ran up and hung a congratulatory pendant around my neck. I crumpled to the grass and cried like a baby—yup—from the elation of accomplishing something I hadn't known was possible for me.

Lisa and Mary found me right away, which seemed miraculous in a crowd of thousands that, yes, finished long before the 2 hours and 14 minutes it took me. Blubbering on the grass, I assured them I was not hurt, just amazed that I'd made it. I thanked them for believing in me when I didn't even believe in myself—for holding that container for me to step into.

This experience expanded my vision of what I think *I* can do, and what I think *others* can do.

Your Turn . . .

Ask yourself:

Where in your life do you stop yourself for fear of not being able to complete the task, or fear of not doing it well enough?

What would it take to find out if you can do "it"? (Run a race, write that poem, or sing on stage?)

What would you attempt to do if you knew you could not fail?

What would happen if you accomplished it?

Take your time. Be in the discomfort of knowing that you want to do this but are afraid to try. I sure was. The outcome is life changing. I promise!

Chapter 11

Choosing Love or Fear

In the late '80s I had a life-altering trip to California. I landed in San Francisco and made my way north to the beautiful town of Sausalito. I had read a book about a school where children were taught to live in joy, in the present moment—even with their terminal illnesses. These children learned that no matter what their life circumstances were, they had a choice to experience peace or conflict, love or fear.

"No way! How was this possible?" I wondered. My breaths deepened and my heart expanded over the possibility of such a sanctuary. The concept alone was mind-blowing, and I was deeply moved even before I arrived.

As I drove up in my little red rental car, I noted feelings of intimidation. But I didn't give myself the time needed to draw understanding from that emotion. Instead, I hopped out of the car and knocked on the door of The Center for Attitudinal Healing. Patty, a perky volunteer, greeted me. She gave me a bit of the history of the center and its founders, Jerry Jampolsky and Diane Cirincione, and explained their overarching message: *At every moment, each of us chooses how we are going to live, no matter what our life circumstances.*

I remember Patty having to leave the room for a moment, which gave me a welcome bit of time to digest something that felt indigestible. While I was intrigued by the concept of the center, I wondered how it was possible. If I had a terminal illness, I couldn't envision hanging out with other sick people; even if I did, we certainly wouldn't be joyful. Or would we? Part of me was ready for the tour, but part of me was not.

Patty returned swiftly as promised, and she led me down a hallway. I could already hear the voices and laughter emerging from a classroom. We stopped at the doorway and she explained that it was time for the children's art class. I stood in the doorway as one little girl ran up, said hello, hugged me, and ran off. The classroom was filled with laughing children—some drawing, some painting—with seemingly not a care in the world. Some had incurable cancers, others had heart conditions, and others had prognoses I wasn't aware of.

These children were happy. Genuinely happy. They laughed, painted, and played as though there was only *this* moment. And though I believed the concept of joy could only be found in the present moment, seeing it acted out before me was astounding.

I was humbled. I felt vulnerable. I wondered how this scene would have had such an impact if it was something I already believed—that we *do* choose how we live each moment, despite our circumstances. Was it because it appeared to be such an extreme example? Was the Universe asking me to examine my own life and look at where I didn't live this truth I professed to believe? Was I afraid that if I were in their situation, I wouldn't embrace my own teaching?

This life-changing moment moved me to tears. When the tour ended and we said our good-byes, I remember aimlessly walking through the streets of Sausalito for what felt like hours.

As I walked, I came to truly see how much time and energy I was using to focus on things like the fear of the unknown, the fear of the future, and the fear of who I am not. And, in that moment, I was gifted with the new reminder of choices. New ways of living each and every moment, as though each moment is a gift—whether we have one more day, or decades more, to live.

That day I promised to embrace gratitude and live into my sacred journey more than ever. I became a student, and I will be forever grateful. I've never looked at life the same since my visit to The Center for Attitudinal Healing.

"Is there life before death?"
—Jon Kabat-Zinn

10 Things People Regret the Most Before They Die

After hosting many gatherings on the subject of living powerfully in the now, I've compiled a list of common regrets as written by clients who were asked to imagine that they had just days left to live.

1. I wish I had lived more in the moment and appreciated what I had, instead of what I did not have.
2. I wish I had traveled more.
3. I wish I had spent more time trusting my intuition.
4. I wish I had pursued my dreams more.
5. I wish I hadn't been so afraid of failure.
6. I wish I had looked fear in the eye and done "it" anyway!
7. I wish I hadn't held back when I wanted to express love to family and friends.
8. I wish I had spoken up more and asked for what I needed.

9. I wish I had worried less about what others think about me.
10. I wish I had known that I was enough already!

Your Turn . . .

Imagine that you have just days to live.

What would be some of your biggest regrets? What will you do differently today?

1. _____
2. _____
3. _____

Here are a few of mine: (I'm sweating just thinking about this.)

- I wish I had grabbed courage by the balls and put myself out there more.
- I wish I had spoken up more in school.
- I wish I'd told my friends I loved them more often.

How might we live into our lists? It's not too late.

The Other Shoe

Is it really going to drop?
Shall I deprive myself this joy?
Shall I guard myself?
Play it safe?
Can the elation of this moment really cause me to fall?

I'll tell you what I'm going to do
I'm going to live balls-to-the-wall
Fast, then slow
Wildly in love
Heart wide open.

I will dance with Courage
Have the audacity to shine
Fall and get back up again.

When life ebbs and flows
I will hug Grace
Hold the hand of Hope
Gather my tribe
Find home base in both my shoes.

—Elizabeth Trinkaus

Chapter 12

The Stories We Tell Ourselves

Years ago I attended a Hay House Writer's Conference in Chicago with some of my favorite mentors: Nancy Levin, Mike Dooley, and Reid Tracy. Nancy asked us to do a simple exercise that gave us complete permission to write with abandon, move our energy, and *just see* what happens. The instructions were as follows: Take out a piece of paper and pen, begin each sentence with *"I remember,"* and stop after 10 minutes.

I said to myself, "Really, only 10 minutes? What am I supposed to discover in 10 minutes? I'll barely get started!" And here's a sampling of what happened . . .

I Remember

I remember being eight years old, living in my beautiful Connecticut home.
I remember I was handed a duffel bag, being told we were leaving.
I remember not knowing where I was going, sometimes feeling out of control.
I remember my dad at the helm, my mom saying "yes."
I remember riding across the Tappan Zee Bridge with my two older brothers and our three dogs.
I remember a journey with no direction, feeling as though all of life is unpredictable.
I remember becoming a chameleon, wanting desperately to fit in.

I remember eighth grade in the rural South, my first interracial school.
I remember observing the Blacks and Whites, how they made themselves different when they got around each other.
I remember making friends with the Black girls, and the White boys hating me.
I remember being called "Moose" when I entered a room, and thinking it was because I was from the North.
I remember realizing it was because I had crossed a line, a line I didn't know existed.

I remember feeling intuitive, playing myself down.
I remember empathing others, and hiding my gift.
I remember sensing people's pain, and knowing it was not my own.

I remember God, and how "Godly" leaders fell.
I remember being disillusioned, feeling heartbroken.
I remember still believing, but trying to do it on my own.

I remember thinking I had to work for love, never feeling enough.
I remember studying counseling in college, wanting to make sense of it all.
I remember asking for help, beginning to find direction.

I remember uncovering huge insecurities, and learning they were not who I really am.
I remember learning that my past does not dictate my future.
I remember beginning to align with who I am, and being called to her journey.

I remember observing the power of what happens when one learns to love herself.

I remember being willing to embrace the wild journey with helpers.

I remember coming home, and desiring to live every day as though it matters.

The exercise was cathartic. It was eye-opening. It was somehow thrilling and scary at the same time. I had been given permission to spill my guts, and some of the contents proved mysterious. The exercise gave me full permission to notice the stories I tell myself from my past, and most importantly, how to switch stations. (And yes, I went over the 10-minute mark.)

I highly recommend this exercise to you. It offers another way for you to shine the light on old stories that might need to be rewritten for your powerful present.

If Doubting Dotty—*who will judge and compare*—shows up, shift to compassion and breathe deeply. You will accomplish two exercises in one. Believing Betty is always cheering you on!

Your Turn...

Take 10 minutes to write as many statements as you can, beginning with:

I remember ...

I remember ...

I remember ...

I remember ...

I remember ...

I remember ...

Old Stories/New Stories

Let's go deeper and really define "old stories" and "new stories."

An **old story** is a narrative we tell ourselves, based on past experiences. Example: If a parent was emotionally unavailable, the old story could sound like: *"I have to work for love,"* or *"I am unlovable."* Or if an environment was unsafe, the old story could sound like: *"Life is not safe."*

These stories, though they may have been true and served a purpose back then, can manifest in our adult life, even if we are safe now and, of course, lovable.

A **new story** is a positive story we choose to tell ourselves now, in the present moment. Your new story is a true statement based on a combination of your wisdom and new tools. An example of a new story could be: *"Their lack of expressing love, or their not being available, has nothing to do with my value and worth. It just felt like it did. I acknowledge that and affirm that I am lovable. I choose to no longer work for love."*

New stories can be very challenging to write and own in the beginning. We merge with the justified anger of the old story and can ride that intoxicating tale for a long time. It's so damn familiar! The ego whispers that it would rather be *right* (and hold on to the old story) than be *happy* (and let it go).

"*But this is what happened to me!*" we insist, and wear it like a banner. It can really keep us stuck. Giving up the *old* means we can no longer use our past as an excuse to *not* move forward. Let me say that again:

Giving up the old means we can no longer use our past as an excuse to not move forward.

I am in no way diminishing what happened in your past. I am, however, proclaiming that YOU ARE NOT YOUR PAST, and your past does *not* have to dictate your future. You are new every day. And having the courage to own a new story—well, it's transformational.

When we are ready to forgive and willing to let go of an old story, a new story has the potential to radically empower our lives. Forgiveness does not mean condoning an event; rather, it is the power to set oneself free.

Need help letting go? Promise yourself that you will get all the support you need to move through the places where you feel really stuck. There are lots of great coaches out there who are trained to assist you and hold the place for incredible healing.

The Power to Shift

The stories we tell ourselves can empower us or keep us chained in cycles of constant struggle.
They are like a low-volume radio station always playing in the background.
We keep the stories alive—until we don't anymore.
And when we realize that we have the power to shift the messages that are not relevant anymore,
We can fly.

—Elizabeth Trinkaus

Chapter 13

Real-Life Clients' Old/New Stories

I am so grateful to be assisting others in their journeys toward understanding their old stories, rewriting them, and claiming their new stories. Following are some examples of how clients have transformed from old stories into new ones. Names have been changed and permission graciously granted in hopes that their stories might inspire yours.

While each client session is unique, there is a common thread of grounding—when we get out of our own way and align with *who we really are*—that creates inner shifts and lasting results. This is done with the gift of intuition, the power of guided visualizations, focusing on our feet (yes, our feet), and separating out from the stuff that weighs us down and continually takes us out. Something magical—yes, magical—happens when we take the time and energy to do these simplest of steps to get back home.

Home to who we really are . . .

Before we look at some real-life stories, let's take a moment and do my clients' very favorite *grounding exercise*. It's a favorite, perhaps, because after people do this a few times, they are able to go back to it quickly and reap its great benefits.

The key to this grounding exercise is getting us out of our heads and all the way into our feet. It's the first step to allow us to experience a *mental recess*.

Let's do this together:

1. Take three deep breaths—in through the nose and out through the mouth.
2. Relax your shoulders.
3. Bring your focus to your feet by wiggling your toes.

You're doing it! A mental recess that is the beginning of feeling grounded.

Practice this in traffic, in long lines at the grocery store, or when you are on a stressful call. It will soon become second nature. It's quick, it works, and the mental recess is such a welcome relief.

Patty

Patty was a manager at a Fortune 500 company in New York City and had a two-hour commute each way from New Jersey. The company flew me in to meet with Patty because her stress had gotten so out of control that it was beginning to affect her work.

I'll never forget our first session. She quickly told me that her life was 150 percent work, and she had no time for herself. She didn't sleep well at night; the stress had caused her to start smoking; and she was eating crappy fast food every day because that's all she had time for.

After our initial session, she began moving through the guilt she felt because she rarely took moments for herself anymore. We scheduled a series of phone sessions, and Patty began to uncover a belief system (old story) that caused her to feel that her worth and identity were completely wrapped up in her work. Eventually she realized, "Of course there's no time for me! I tell myself I have to take every call, keep my office door open, and say 'yes' to everyone who asks for help. I'm effective, but I'm miserable—and I'm not sure it's worth it."

The realization that her essence and worth are separate from her job was a huge epiphany. Patty began to wonder what it would be like to listen to what *she* needs and to have the audacity to make herself a priority!

Her logical mind knew this would be a good thing—and of course she would recommend the same for a friend; but it felt foreign to her. She wondered if she could still do good work. Feelings of "Do I deserve this?" surfaced.

I reminded her to take baby steps, to make small changes over time that would potentially generate amazing results. She began closing her office door for short periods during the day to catch up on emails and phone calls.

She confessed that this almost killed her at first. She knew people *needed* her out there. But she breathed. She began listening to herself—a novel idea in and of itself—and she discovered that taking breaks throughout the day made her less stressed *and* more effective.

She realized she could survive saying "no" to certain things, although she occasionally cringed inside. The biggest life-changer was making the distinction between *who she is* and *what she does*. Patty was astonished that she was getting things accomplished, putting in fewer hours, *and* feeling better!

She called me months later and said, "You're not going to believe this! I got a bonus and a raise! How is that possible?" She went on to report that she found an apartment much closer to her office, quit smoking, was eating more healthily, *and* was losing weight!

Old Story: My worth equals what I do. I must work 60+ hours and try to please everyone. Surely I'll feel I am good enough soon?

New Story: I AM already enough. I matter. I give myself permission to take care of myself *and* do good work in the world.

Fran

Fran was 53. When we met, she told me about her life and what she hoped to accomplish. Though she was good at starting project after project, she inevitably stopped herself with fears of failure. She was paralyzed, left wondering if any of her ideas were good enough to see through to completion.

I explained to her that we all have subconscious beliefs about who we think we are and how we show up in the world. And, when a pattern continually repeats itself in one's life, there is almost always an "old story" there that we are telling ourselves. At this point in my work with clients, I find the most beneficial next step is a guided visualization (GV). I suggested Fran allow me to lead her through a GV and see where it might take us.

Just as it sounds, a GV lets us escape; it gets us out of the space in our minds where we keep telling ourselves the same thing, the same story, over and over again. As we escape our minds, we have the opportunity to fully inhabit our bodies. A guided visualization is another type of mental recess that helps us get grounded.

I explained a favorite image I have of kids in a classroom who hear the bell for recess—how the door flies open and kids litter the playground in a matter of seconds. We, as adults, are in desperate need of "recess," but instead we often pretend we are machines—and we just continue to motor forward. Again, here is your opportunity to be fully in your body, to relax, and to connect with that inner wisdom that is always there, waiting for you to slow down and listen.

Fran closed her eyes. I asked her to imagine the warm light of sunshine showering her body, all the way to her feet. She wiggled her toes as requested and felt grounded. She noted that she already felt better. We talked about the pattern that kept recurring for her, and she proceeded to take more deep breaths. She remembered that when she was four, her older sister attempted to teach her to write. Out of sheer frustration, her sister yelled, *"You'll never get this!"* (old story).

In that moment, Fran realized that throughout her whole life, every time she started a new project she felt the fear and angst of possibly *"not getting it,"* which left her feeling insecure and never enough. This brought up huge issues of low self-esteem and provoked anxiety attacks. She would put off projects, and always made sure to avoid certain people who she thought were going to make her feel this way.

She sat in amazement with the discovery of how this memory had affected her for her whole life up to that moment. She acknowledged where it came from and got that she was *not* that story. This clarity was more than a relief. For Fran, it was a mystery solved, an opportunity for empowerment, and an enormous feeling of freedom.

Then came her new story. It sounded like, "I've got this," "deep breaths," "I can do this."

"This is amazing!" she stated—so simple and so powerful. "It's as if the clouds parted for me and I can see where I've been blocking myself."

The next step was for Fran to turn this into a daily practice.

Did the old story reappear? Absolutely. But with her courage and her willingness to shine light on it, it no longer had power over her. It was no longer lurking in the shadows and stealing her confidence and creativity. She knew the next half of her life was going to look and feel a lot different! And, in fact, it does . . .

I met with Fran months later. She told me she'd started her own retail business and she had three people working for her. She said when the old story reappears, she takes a deep breath and reminds herself that *she's got this*, which shifts her mind from fear to more empowerment and helps her to live in the present.

Old Story: "You'll never get this!"

New Story: "I've got this," "deep breaths," "I can do this."

Tanya

Tanya was overweight—by about 75 pounds. When she came to me, she told me something I'd heard other overweight women say: Being fat made her invisible, and that made her feel safe.

Tanya's troubles started when she was 12, and her older teenage brother began to sexually and physically abuse her. Her parents didn't acknowledge it, though she suspected her mother may have known about it but felt powerless to stop it. So, Tanya started eating to numb the pain—and as she started to gain weight, she thought perhaps being fat might save her. If she looked unattractive to her brother, maybe the abuse would stop.

As she hid herself in food and books, and eventually moved away to college where she was out of physical danger from her brother, she continued to suffer. The abuse continued to affect her on such an emotional level that she continued to want to hide. She carried the shame—and the weight—and this took away her ability to feel any kind of value whatsoever. She felt "devalued."

When I met her, Tanya was ready for change. She came to a retreat with other women, where we worked on aligning with WHO we are. Later, as a private client, she told me her story—which explained why she felt as bad as she did, and how she didn't know feeling differently was even a possibility. She didn't feel her value or worth; she didn't know that she was okay and already enough. Through the process of hearing her old story and separating herself from it, she took the first steps toward the possibility of owning her value, owning her worth.

Tanya didn't have to live under the weight of the past with those old stories. She learned about self-compassion, and began to love herself despite her past. She used affirmations, and declared every day, "I AM ENOUGH." She also worked on new thought processes to love herself. She became conscious of what she was telling herself and began shifting from the negative self-talk. Choosing self-compassion helped her to feel safe in her own skin—something she had been unable to feel for more than thirty years.

Tanya shifted to living in the present (new story) instead of the past (old story). The more she did it, the more she loved it, and she began to drop the weight—50 pounds. She realized she didn't have to hide from something that wasn't happening now. She didn't have to hide who she was. In fact, as she lost weight, she gained a greater sense of who she really was.

She started her own business, continued to lose excess weight, and is now—20 years later—in a loving relationship. Tanya's unhappy past affected her self-esteem so much that she used to choose only men who were judgmental toward her. As she learned to be kind to herself, she started to attract partners who were also kind and loving. Today she is healthy, happy, and thriving.

By shifting out of her old story and into a new one, Tanya learned to love herself, align with her worth, and be filled by her gifts. She lost 75 pounds *and* has kept it off for years.

Old Story: Food makes me feel safe and comforts me.

New Story: I *am* safe. I make me safe. I remind myself to live powerfully in the present. I'm never going back to my childhood situation. I create stability for me.

Tina

Tina was in a miserable marriage with a man who abused her verbally and, at times, physically. Rather than question it, however, she thought on some level she deserved her husband's anger and wrath, and she felt too disconnected from herself to speak up. After he left her for another woman, Tina felt both unworthy and abandoned. She started attending my retreats and became open to the possibility of learning concepts of loving herself and accepting that she was worthy of a healthy relationship.

When she came to her first workshop, Tina began to mourn who she'd been in her marriage. She realized she didn't know she could have, should have, and *deserved* to leave the marriage. Until she understood that she was enough, just looking back and talking about the marriage was a challenge for her. But she was dedicated to working through it and chose to write and read affirmations every day that said, "I am deserving of a loving, healthy partner. I love me."

She began to believe wholeheartedly in the law of attraction—that what you put out there is what you'll get back—and exactly a year and a half later she met the man of her dreams. He was a loving man, whom she fell in love with—and now they are happily married. They travel, and they love life together.

Tina lives in gratitude every day, knowing she was able to go from feeling so desperately NOT ENOUGH to being in such a solid, loving, great relationship. And living in the reality that she is ENOUGH ALREADY.

Tina doesn't recognize the person she used to be; she says she can't believe she was that woman. She looks back and thinks: "OH MY GOD, that poor girl!"

Changing her story has truly changed her life.

Old Story: I feel empty. Not enough. I must keep the peace.

New Story: I am lovable. I know I deserve a loving relationship. I am worthy (wow). I've learned to love me.

Your Turn...

What's your old story?

If you are having a hard time determining an old story, think of something that challenges you—perhaps being interviewed, speaking in front of a group, going on a date, owning your truth. What are you telling yourself during these times?

One of my "old stories" was feeling like I was never *enough*. This played out in career choices, romantic choices—all choices, really. It negatively affected everything. And I was always trying to do more, be more. When I slowed down and looked inward, the pattern was not difficult to discover. My new story title is simple: "I am more than enough, in all my imperfections" . . . and it is a continual process of remembering. Again, the rewards are great.

Trust the process. Notice. Listen. Is there a negative story that potentially feels true and has a way of replaying in your life?

Remind yourself that you are not this old story. It no longer has power over you, and it will not define how you gauge your true worth.

Look at some old stories that might be negatively affecting your journey. (Get support in having someone walk you through them whenever you are in need.)

Take a deep breath. Relax your shoulders. Close your eyes and be open to hearing an old story that has been playing.

Old Story: *I am not deserving of* _____.
I am not lovable because _____.
No wonder I can't _____.

Take another breath. The old story will likely be very familiar, so familiar that you have owned it as your truth.

I breathe . . . I am willing to let them go. Knowing that my new story has the potential to transform my life.

Now release that old story. Watch it disappear . . . like a puff of smoke.

Imagine a new story now, one that frees you to BE the person you'd like to be, and DO the amazing things you'd like to do.

New Story: *The past has no hold over me. I live in the NOW. I deserve love. I am* _____, *and I can do* _____. *I am already enough.*

★

Following is space for you to record your shift from old story to new. Imagine your life as a fresh canvas awaiting your new design. Be bold and grab lots of brushes and bright colors!

Old Story:

New Story:

Put Your New Story on Repeat

The more you remind yourself of your new stories, the more potent they will feel. If you put your new stories on repeat, their results will show up in your life in tangible ways—you might find greater joy and ease, and less stress and dissatisfaction. It's a journey. An amazing one. Live the miracle that you are.

Your Turn . . .

"Top five" new-story affirmations

Now take some time and write your "top five" new-story affirmations. Examples might include:

It's safe to shine my light.

I am safe. I will never abandon me.

I draw wonderful people and experiences into my life.

I am loved and lovable.

My best is enough.

My "top five" new-story affirmations:

1.

2.

3.

4.

5.

Chapter 14

Positive Chalk Talk

While camping at a nearby lake and walking with my pups, I ran into a bunch of young boys writing with chalk on the pavement. I could hear their conversations as I slowly approached and could tell the difference between those who wanted to be cool and those who marched to a different drumbeat.

One kid wrote, "If you can read this, you are stupid." Another kid crossed that out and wrote, "If you can read this, you are awesome. Awesome, awesome, awesome."

I was taken by the kid who chose the high road—his courage to choose "awesome" in the midst of his friends, going against the other boy's "stupid." I walked past and acknowledged him with a smile and a nod.

How might we access and be reminded of our awesomeness every day? What would happen if we did?

Several years ago, I presented a motivational talk to 7th graders at St. Mary's School in Raleigh, North Carolina. We ended the presentation with an activity I call "Positive Chalk Talk." I gave all 70 students a stick of chalk, and because it was raining and we couldn't do this exercise outside, I also gave them poster board to write on. I then asked them what they would like to see and read while they were walking down a sidewalk.

Without any hesitation, they swiftly began writing: "You are loved," "You are enough," "You are awesome," "Great job," "Go for it," etc.

I was amazed, but not surprised. My heart was full and I encouraged them to continue creating Positive Chalk Talk for themselves and for others who will smile inside and out when they read these awesome messages.

You Did a Great Job Today

When I speak to corporate groups, I ask them, "How many of you walked out of your office in the last month and said to yourself, 'I did a great job today'?" I get lots of giggles, and seldom do I see a raised hand. We are more familiar with thinking about what we *didn't* do instead of what we *did*.

There will always be a to-do list. Try focusing on what you did do and watch how those thoughts create a shift in how you experience your evening. This simple shift has proven to make family time, free time, and friends time so much richer.

We all need reminders. Be sure to download your free poster (designed by my big bro Mark Trinkaus), and read it every day: YOU DID A GREAT JOB TODAY!

Find it at www.pinnacleview.net/coaching.

> *When you arise in the morning, think of what a precious privilege it is to be alive—to breathe, to think, to enjoy, to love.*
> —Marcus Aurelius

Your Turn . . .

What kind of messages are you leaving for yourself and for others throughout your day?

Chapter 15

The Backpack

What does it mean to walk with a lighter spirit? To be aware of the weight we carry, the stories we store away, the light we withhold from ourselves...

The Backpack

It's imaginary.
It's heavy. Like bricks.
You may not have noticed it.
Until now.
It contains all those things you were taught to "take on."

As women, we inherit the skill of absorbing everything around us.
We find ourselves walking around with the backpack open, and the contents increase.
Perhaps we're conscious of some of it, while the rest is just habitual stuffing.
We all do it, but do we have to?
It's heavy. It's cumbersome. It's tiring.

Why do we carry this pack and all its stuff?
Because we inherited the my-value-and-worth-are-based-on-doing-for-everyone-else story from all the preceding generations.

We innately "care," but do we need to "wear" all the stuff?
Does caring have to mean wearing?
Does caring mean we wear the multitude of questions with no answers? All the unknowns?
The answer is NO.

When we "take it on," we find ourselves "taken out."
When we wear these burdens, we find we are exhausted, depleted, and depressed . . . with a heap of resentfulness.

Is it possible—with a little practice—we can learn to still "care," but not "wear" it? The answer is YES.
A huge relief, and beneficial for all.

—Elizabeth Trinkaus

Your Turn . . .

The backpack exercise

1. Imagine a big open backpack on your back.
   Stop.
   Notice.
   Breathe.
   What's in your backpack right now?

Common things in one's backpack might include: guilt for taking time for yourself, issues with work, family problems, fear of the unknown, relationship troubles, grief, shame, job uncertainties, money, health concerns, resentment, and just plain overwhelm.

Notice. Does it feel heavy? Are your shoulders weighted down? Is your neck tight? Take a few minutes to write down what's in your backpack:

As you inventoried your backpack, you may have noticed a plethora of burdens—yours and those belonging to others. All are equally valid. I'm not suggesting you pretend they don't exist. But I am offering an effective tool to perhaps shift how you feel.

In the following steps, I will give you the grand opportunity to make *space* between you and the backpack, between you and its contents.

Space is your friend. Space is a healer. It's a perspective changer.

2. Now that you've identified the backpack and its contents, allow yourself to feel them. Perhaps you'll notice it really does weigh you down. Perhaps you'll notice your shoulders are heavy and your neck is tight. Perhaps you'll notice you've been holding your breath.

3. Be open to giving yourself permission to take that backpack off. What does it mean to give yourself permission? Perhaps it means exploring the questions: Who am I without the backpack? Have I told myself it is my identity to take it on? Will I lose my value, be less loved? (Notice your thoughts, any resistance. Resistance is fine—not fun, but fine. Let yourself look. Let yourself hear. There's no blame. Just breathe.)

Room for thoughts:

4. Envision placing the backpack on the floor, and then breathe. There is you, and there is the backpack with all its belongings. There is physical space between you and it. Notice how that feels. What is it like to have space between you and the backpack? Perhaps your shoulders are lighter. It may feel weird.

    Record your feelings:

5. Next, place an imaginary warm cloak over your shoulders and breathe . . .

Yes, breathe. If you've identified heavy burdens in the backpack, your shoulders are used to the feeling of something being there. Notice any thoughts that arise. Don't believe all of them. Especially the ones that say you should do more, be more, carry more . . . that you are nothing without the backpack. Be patient. Hang in there. Remember, you get to choose the thoughts you listen to.

6. Allow yourself to feel the range of sensations. Be open to feeling relief. You might notice you are more effective not wearing the backpack. You may well have more energy and joy. You might be physically lighter and taking deeper breaths. Freeing yourself gives you access to your wisdom, intuition, and strength.

When you choose what to put in your backpack—and what to leave out—the obligatory messages (the shoulds, musts, and what ifs) dissipate, and you return to your heart space.

7. Once you have allowed yourself to remove the backpack, its contents appear different. All those unknowns are not screaming so loudly for answers. All that weight did not make you more valuable. Again, the contents are real and require your attention, but creating space between you and them allows for a new perspective, a new response, deeper breaths, more grace and ease . . .

Perhaps when you put the backpack down, you *are* more yourself, and you will learn to really like you. (I promise that you will.)

Every time you do this exercise, you have the opportunity to release stress, recharge, and realize you are already enough.

Congratulations!

It's Not Gone Yet

But, you ask, what do I do if the backpack comes back?

The backpack WILL come back. Not because you didn't do a great job, but because you're used to it being there. We all are. It's just a pattern. Continue to be conscious. Notice when it returns. Remind yourself that wearing it doesn't help anyone.

Take it off... again. Take it off every hour, every day, with every breath. The more you do this, the easier it will get. Trust me. It will lighten your load.

What If I'm Too Resistant?

Resistance is common. Sometimes it looks like blinders, sometimes it looks like moving even faster, or maybe it looks like taking on even more. Change makes us vulnerable. And we often don't welcome traversing those trails.

Be brave. Remember why you are doing this and that you are worth it (even if you're not "feeling" it). Practice. Baby steps. Imagine how good you will feel running... without a backpack.

Your Turn...

How did it feel when you took your "backpack" off?

When the backpack reappears—and it will: Are you willing to take it off again, and again, until it stays gone?

Are you willing to get used to the freedom of not carrying it, and *own* your worth completely separate from it?

Because you're already enough *(wink)*!

Chapter 16

The Audacity to Shine

This is my favorite poem. It reminds you to own your courage and shine your light.

The Lion

The ivy did not scare her,
The large trees were her friend,
but the day she heard the water,
she knew she could not pretend.

In the forest, she could no longer hide,
protection it was no more,
time to emerge to the water,
Come ... for what she came here for.

She heard messages in the water,
its wisdom was her friend,
no longer was she to be in hiding,
it was time to breathe and transcend.

The Lion sat waiting by her pool,
as if a daily event,
he smiled as she emerged,
knowing her time of hiding was well spent.

They smiled as they met,
knowing each other by heart,
she still breathed a sigh of relief,
accepting the courage he would impart.

Being in the full sunlight,
did not hurt her shielded eyes,
She was reassured,
that it was her day to fly.

No drums, no horns were needed,
the open heart was plenty enough,
she saw with new ears and eyes,
and was no longer trailing her stuff.

Her reflection in the pool was great comfort,
her efforting fell to the ground,
the relief was a bit of a mystery,
but she knew she had finally come home.

There was finally, truly great distance,
from the souls that were scared of her light,
she knew that this fresh pool of water,
was to heal her and offer insight.

When she stopped she could hear the great messages,
that once were a daily event,
she reveled in her old gift,
and how her new future would be spent.

So cheers to the Lion who brought courage,
the holders of space I adore,
to gratitude, my ancient great teacher,
to the opening of hearts and big doors.

To the truth-teller by the pool of water,
to the gifts so graciously bestowed,
to the angels and helpers all over,
to the light she has the courage to show.

—Elizabeth Trinkaus

I had the privilege of teaching a course at the renowned Chautauqua Institute in New York. My topic: The Audacity to Shine. I chose the topic because I, and so many others whom I work with, have been accustomed to dimming our lights. If we are not paying attention, we tone it down a bit . . . or maybe even a lot.

What is shining? Shining is showing up, speaking up, slowing down enough to know what you need, and asking the Universe for it. In our Chautauqua class, all of us agreed that we hold ourselves back sometimes, for fear of what others will think.

Perhaps you've been told, "Don't get too big for your britches," or "Who do you think you are?"—and you've played yourself down because you don't want others to feel uncomfortable. Perhaps you have silenced yourself when your soul wanted to speak up, or you charged less than you knew you deserved because you didn't want to upset anyone. Or perhaps you didn't take action because you were afraid of the unknown . . .

I know I have deliberately turned down my light. Often.

There's good news. By being aware, conscious of the stories we tell ourselves, we all have the opportunity to shift from Doubting Dotty to Believing Betty. We can have full permission to drag those non-shiny messages to the delete bin. And the more we practice letting go of the old negative scripts, the easier it is to shine.

Are you ready to let go of playing small? I know I am! We have many shiny new stories to live into!

Marianne Williamson, in her book *A Return to Love*, says it best:

Our deepest fear is not that we are inadequate.
Our deepest fear is that we are powerful beyond measure.
It is our light, not our darkness, that most frightens us.

That reminder never gets old. Thank you, Marianne . . . fantastic!

At our last women's beach retreat a participant said, "I *am* full of myself! What else would I want to be full of?" Giving yourself permission to be you, love you, and shine is the greatest gift you can give yourself and the world. And the world desperately needs your shininess!

Another Old Story

At a young age I was often made fun of for overusing the word "fantastic." Okay, I pronounced it more like fan-TAS-tic! I used it a lot. Not just because I'm quite fond of the word, but because I felt it. I felt it in my bones.

I remember deciding it best to play myself down and hold back my exuberance, because the pain of being made fun of outweighed the joy (at that time).

Ringing in my ears was, *"If you use superlatives all the time, what are you going to say when something really is fanTAStic?"*

Ouchhh! That one stung. I immediately archived it into the library of old stories: *"Don't shine too brightly."* And I had notable moments of "dimming" for the comfort of those around me and myself.

While the providers of hurtful comments—friends, family, or teachers—usually meant no harm, those of us on the receiving end have the tendency to take these messages to heart, and to dim a little of who we really are. Until we are *not* that kind of girl anymore.

We are on a journey of waking up and longing for our shining presence.

Not shining is like living oceanfront with the windows closed and the blinds pulled. It's like Pink Floyd playing with the mute button pushed. It's like sitting with noise-canceling earphones on at your favorite piano bar.

Shining, however, is like mustering the courage to BE YOU and releasing the judgments around you, and in you.

Shining is opening those oceanfront windows and blinds, taking "Shine On You Crazy Diamond" off mute, and cranking up the volume. It's singing, laughing out loud, and unapologetically showing up. When you give yourself permission to soar that high, you will always want more (of your essence). And you will never go back.

I recently offered my "Living in Balance" presentation to a Fortune 100 company. While being introduced, I was expecting the predictable fear wave, *I-hope-they-like-me*, to rise from my stomach and land in my throat. That day, however, it never did. Hmmmm, I thought. This stuff really works.

Practicing the shiny tools and being willing to let all the people in the room have a hundred different opinions about me was freeing. Really freeing.

Will the fear wave reappear? Yes, it will—but less often. And, giving myself permission to shine and be myself in the midst of the discomfort is the greatest gift of all!

For generations so many of us have been taught to viciously compare ourselves, to discount our incredible uniqueness, and to *not* be who we are. And now we are changing the game. Changing the rules.

It's time to shine.

And trust me, you will have plenty of opportunity to "practice."

Shuga, Don't Shrink

I was visiting my 94-year-old friend Mary, who'd been a proper New York schoolteacher in her day. I walked in smiling, expecting her usual greeting, "Hi, shuga."

But not that day. She looked at me and said, *"You like those fuc#ing boots, don't you?"* These were words I had never heard come out of her pretty mouth before. WOW!

I paused. A long pause. The "old me" who wanted to play it safe, to be accepted, wished to say something like, "What, these old things?" while simultaneously making a mental note to *n-e-v-e-r* wear these boots here again.

But that day I stopped. I breathed. I refused to dim my light. And with a crack in my voice, I replied, *"Yes, I do* love *these fuc#ing boots."*

Oooops, did I just say that to my elderly friend? Oh . . . yes, I did! And in that moment, I knew I had broken a spell. A spell I had cast on myself years ago, one that loomed in the shadows every time I wanted to shine but it felt unsafe.

Mary grinned and replied, "You like to stand out, don't you?"

I answered, "I like to be me." (I noted I was taking in a breath that was deeper than ever before, *and* my heart rate was off the charts.)

In that moment, I had granted myself permission to shine—I had the audacity to shine in my favorite brown-and-turquoise cowgirl boots! I refused to painfully shrink and slither back down the four flights of stairs of that retirement home in my offensive boots. I released the notion that I should "tone it down a little" or perhaps should have "known better" in the first place.

It's not that I will never feel like slithering again, but now I know I will slither *less*. And if I feel the urge to pull back, I will remember that the momentary discomfort of disapproval is far less painful than the feeling of self-betrayal.

Hello, Sacred Journey

Her breaths are deep,
Her eyes are wide,
Her heart so open,
Her antenna so high.

She feels God in all things,
Grace abounds,
"Is this heaven?"
No one uttered a sound.

"It can be," one replied,
"Hell no," said another,
In the midst of the confusion,
She began to take cover.

"You can shine here," one proclaimed,
"It's a threat over there."
A chameleon she became,
The sacred path was nowhere.

She struggled along,
Her antenna high then low,
She wondered what could free her,
And return her great glow.

Through lessons and great teachers,
She is reminded each day,
That it's safe to shine,
And celebrate today.

—Elizabeth Trinkaus

Your Turn . . .

Take the "shine" pledge.

Join me in committing to shine. Is there an area in your life that challenges you in the *Shining Department*? Places where you'd like to show up, speak up, and allow yourself to be vulnerable? Your work, communication, certain relationships, all of the above? (Trust me, I understand.)

Close your eyes. Breathe. Be willing to look and bring light to any dark corners. Fear gets smaller in the light. Courage will find you.

I choose to shine my light more in these areas of my life:

Shine on. We are all in it together!

Chapter 17

Your Happy Place

Ahhhh. Spending time by the water . . . What happens when we do?

For me, it calms the chatter in my head and creates a state of relaxation that perhaps harkens back to when I was in the womb—not that any of us can remember precisely!

When I kick back and relax on my pontoon boat, time seems to stand still and nature appears more accented. By that I mean the eagles generously make themselves present, and the clouds constantly put on a show. My breathing is deeper and my inspiration greater. Being on the water balances the fire within me.

Having the awareness that life is so precious makes me ask: How do I want to live?

The water is truly "my happy place." Identifying *your* happy place(s), and then going there, will draw creativity to your mind, inspiration to your soul, and magnificent fuel to recharge your journey.

Where is your happy place? On the water? In the mountains? Sitting by a riverbank or walking through the woods? Curling up with a good book by a woodstove? Brushing paint on a canvas, riding your horse, dancing and singing, or snipping overgrowth in your garden?

How do you feel when you're in your happy place? Can you find a way to channel those good feelings even when you're not there?

Waiting Makes Us Miss Out

Carly Simon had a hit back in the 1970s, "Anticipation," that is still a good reminder when I'm tempted to forget about the present and instead wait for the future. What happens when we do this? We lose the only "now" we'll ever have. If we take this to the extreme, we might never feel the joy and power of "now," because we're always looking toward—waiting for—some far-off future. It causes us to miss out on what's right in front of us *now*.

Anticipation is makin' me late, is keepin' me waiting . . .
—Carly Simon

Your Turn . . .

Do you find yourself in a constant state of waiting? What are you waiting for?
I am waiting until _____
before I feel _____.

What if you changed your approach and instead embraced the preciousness of this present moment, and then applied the necessary tools to create what you desire? How would that look? Try this simple process.

1. I am present.
2. I am grateful.
3. I create:

(Examples might include: more peace at home, time for me, artwork or poetry, etc.)

Chapter 18

We All Need Reminders

We all need reminders to live in the present, to shift from the old story to the new, to own the miracle that we are today, *and* to remember that we are enough already!

Will Rogers wrote: "Even if you're on the right track, you'll get run over if you just sit there."

For these tools to have amazing results in your life, you need to be reminded of them, and practice them every day.

I have affirming messages in every room of my home. Bathroom included. Oh, in my car also, and on the bumper too!

Over the years, I've had many mentors who have taught me and provided me with reminders of how I can be my best self. I'm guessing you, too, have had many great teachers. Aside from my coach in Santa Barbara—whom I dial often—here are some suggestions for you.

Mike Dooley's "Notes from the Universe"

I met Mike at a workshop when he was just starting his speaking career. What I love about Mike is that he tells his story of being down and out, not knowing how things were going to work, and how he just kept going, refusing to give up. He began writing daily positive-message emails from "The Universe" to encourage others, and now has over a million followers.

The "Notes from the Universe" (NFTU) are funny and fun and so spot-on. Often when I read the NFTU, I feel that the Universe is peeking in my window and delivering the exact message I need that day. Mike travels the world teaching how thoughts become things—and why we should make them good! He also co-teaches the fabulous Hay House Writer's Conference. You can sign up for his daily messages at www.tut.com.

Brené Brown

Brené did a TED talk that reached millions of people. Before I knew who she was, I had several clients ask if I had listened to her talk because we deliver similar messages. Brené's messages of bravery, vulnerability, authenticity, and how we are all so perfectly imperfect resonated deeply within me. It was so familiar and felt like fuel to my soul. I highly recommend her books: *The Gifts of Imperfection* and *Daring Greatly*. I just listened to her new book, *Braving the Wilderness,* on a road trip to Connecticut to see my mom. Okay, I listened to it twice!

Brené reminds us to ask ourselves: *"What is the story I am telling myself about this situation?"* The question has us shifting from unfounded assumptions, accepting our vulnerabilities, and showing up courageously with all our imperfections.

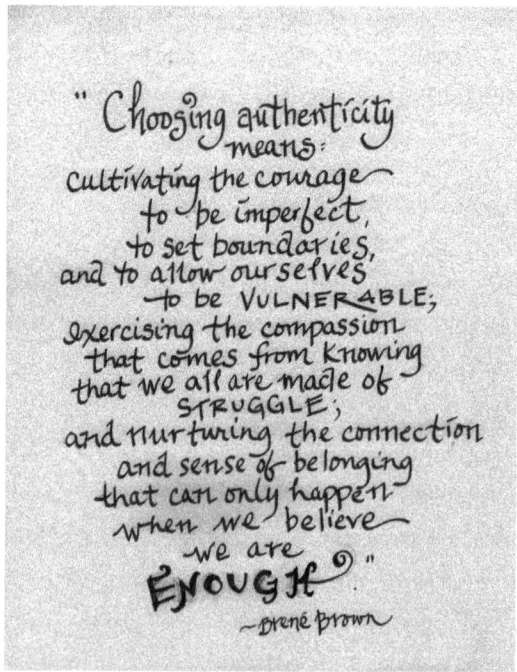

Louise Hay

Louise transitioned to an angel during the writing of this book. She was one of the original pioneers in the teachings of the power of our thoughts, and she will always be the *Affirmation Queen* to me. Affirmations—the self-talk we tell ourselves—create habitual ways of thinking and behaving. Louise had people creating positive affirmations long before they were known to have such a profound impact. She created the Mirror Work exercise, which is a powerful tool to help you learn to love yourself—the greatest gift you can give yourself! That exercise instructs you to look at yourself in the mirror, pause, and say, "I love you."

I've used this exercise numerous times at retreats, and it's more challenging than one might think. Why? Because we're so used to looking in the mirror and focusing on what we don't like about ourselves, and constantly criticizing our bodies. This exercise brings a whole new flavor to that common event, and its benefits are huge. You will become more aware of what you are telling yourself, and you will learn to be kinder to yourself.

This energy of self-love will shift your energy, your vibration, and what you draw to yourself. I've had women break down in tears and tell themselves, "I'm so sorry I've been so hard on you . . . I love you."

Another great reminder that you are enough already! Live the miracle you are today. Don't wait!

I taught the Mirror Work exercise to my friend Zoë, who at the time was only eight. Now when I ask her, "What do you say when you look in the mirror?" she replies, "I love you!"

To begin being kind and loving to yourself at eight years old . . . how fan-TAS-tic!

Mirror Mermaid by Zoë Boardman

Jack Canfield

Jack's mission in life is to help you get from where you are to where you want to be. Many of you know him as the best-selling author of the *Chicken Soup for the Soul* series. His latest book, *The Success Principles*, is a powerful reminder to believe in your dreams and take action to achieve them. I became a certified *Canfield Success Principles* trainer and recently attended a *Mastermind Retreat* at his home in Santa Barbara, California. I refer to *The Success Principles* on a regular basis. Consider grabbing a copy for yourself.

Nancy Levin

I met Nancy at a Hay House Conference years ago. I observed how she managed the speakers and people around her, and had the gift of confidently getting things done. Years later she taught at a Hay House Writer's Conference in Chicago. She had become an author and was helping thousands of others own their stories and put them on paper. I later attended her class "WORTHY: Boost Your Self-Worth to Grow Your Net Worth."

Nancy is gifted in helping others love themselves, believe in themselves, and own their worth. Check out her books, *Jump . . . and Your Life Will Appear* and *The New Relationship Blueprint*.

Super Soul Sunday

I love that Oprah created a magical place in nature where teachers come from all over the world to share their stories and offer specific tools to help us live our best life. I pull up a show when I need a boost to help realign with my highest version, and to get back on track. We all need reminders! And when life gets really challenging, sometimes we even need to be reminded of what we believe.

> *We delight in the beauty of the butterfly, but rarely admit the changes it has gone through to achieve that beauty.*
> —Maya Angelou

Your Tribe

We all need support, and having a safe container where we can dive deeply—and swagger with the certainty that we are ENOUGH already—is priceless! The world needs more sacred spaces for women to be themselves and share their gifts. Create your tribe and focus on *who you are*, instead of who you are not.

Your tribe can be 2, 20, or 2000. It's my honor to provide a step-by-step guide to those interested in creating their own monthly women's gathering. It includes do's and don'ts, my successes and failures, and ready-to-go turnkey curriculum. Contact me at et@pinnacleview.net for more info on how you can create your own tribe and make a difference in the lives of those around you.

Waking Up

It's as though I am waking up from a long sleep . . .
My dream—or should I call it nightmare—was that I constantly tried to be enough, feel enough, but no matter what I did, nothing made it better!
Thank God I am awake.
Thank God I am enough already!

—Elizabeth Trinkaus

Chapter 19

The *Enough Already!* Happy Dance

Congratulations! You have slowed down. You have shown up. You have opened yourself to the possibility that you are already enough, today. You are open to owning the million miracles that potentially accompany such an insight.

You have let go of old stories and are living into the new. You have a full tool kit that will help you shine when you forget, and a strong platform that will catch you if you fall. You have the wisdom to get up again, and the courage that will take you anywhere.

Welcome to your new journey that has you so aware, so empowered, and so grateful to be alive. Remember to call on your angel helpers, your tribe, and know you are never alone. Remember to 86 the mirage, revisit your exercises, notice your shifts, and celebrate the miracle that you are today.

Enough Already! *Yes, you are!*

About the Author

Little Liz with wand, age 5

Elizabeth Trinkaus is the Founder and Chief Inspiration Officer of Pinnacle View, a life-enrichment company. For over 25 years, she has helped thousands of clients around the world take steps to live their best life.

She is a certified workshop leader of the Louise Hay *Heal Your Life* principles, a certified success coach and trainer of the *Canfield Success Principles*, a certified Pre-Cognitive Re-Educator, and holds a BS in counseling. She is the co-author of *Conversations On Success* with Deepak Chopra and others, and *Success Simplified* with Stephen Covey and others.

Elizabeth has been bringing her expertise to corporations, schools, retreats, and individuals. She has the education, experience, and tools that will provide the opportunity for you to accept that you are already enough, followed by the inspiration to manifest those precious dreams. She provides the avenue for you to experience the ultimate human freedom—the freedom that comes from knowing you can design your own life and live into your powerful new story.

After feeling that she was never enough—in school, on dates, at work, and, well, in life—she went on a quest to discover why. She found two things: One, she was not alone; and two, it's possible to bust this life-sucking belief.

Because of Elizabeth's intimate journey of coming face-to-face with her not-enough-ness, she is on a perpetual mission to offer attainable tools for others to own, absorb, and wake up to their worthiness. Her relatable messages will pick you up, inspire you, and set you on a new course.

Elizabeth resides in Chapel Hill, North Carolina, with her life squeeze, Greg, and their two rescue pups.

Acknowledgments

"Thank you!" by Zoë Boardman, age 8

I asked for help, and boy-oh-boy did I receive! My heart is bursting with gratitude for each and every one of you!

Greg Fitts: My love-squeeze. It took me three decades to clear my unworthy old stories in order to attract such a delightful soul. After two decades of playing together, I still remind myself you are real—a clear channel of laughter, lightness, and love.

Mom: My best friend who holds a container of unconditional love that appears super-human. You never wavered in your enthusiasm, despite some of my teenage choices that made you gray before your time.

Dad: My biggest teacher. You believed in miracles and were hugely instrumental in my quest to believe in myself and help others to do the same.

Ted Trinkaus: My big bro! You amaze me with your unconditional love and effortless wisdom. Thanks for saving the wild little Liz (three times).

Mark Trinkaus: My other big bro! I am forever grateful for your channeled gift of graphic design—I love my book cover! Thank you for being my twin (despite those 19 months), my sweet protector, and for all the hours you spent loving and caring about this book.

Elizabeth Brown: My wise and witty editor who is filled with guidance, gifts, and patience! Thank you for all the necessary hand-holding through this birthing process.

Lisa DeLoach: For being my wise, fun play partner and for believing in me *soooo* many times when I did not.

Alana Harndon: For being the most delightful, unwavering cheerleader, accountability coach, retreat chef, and most of all . . . friend.

Ivonne Eiseman: For being my kick-ass coach and intuitive fellow traveler. I can't imagine the journey without you.

Chérie Ndaliko: For our late-night pajama edits and for challenging me to be my greatest.

Linda Love and Pam Petch: For your big love and constant support. I'm so comforted by how you "get" me.

Aubrey Griffith Zill: For being my "adopted" dancing queen, retreat cohort, and bright light in this world.

Dawn Galzerano: For believing in me and my work and reminding me to never dance with doubt. I'm so happy to have found you. Thank you, Gordon!

Pam Rivers: For your wisdom, high visions, and unwavering support.

Laura Ertel: For your gift of seeing things that I didn't, and for your humor through the process.

Zoë Boardman: For being an inspiring young artist and beautiful soul. Thank you for sharing your priceless illustrations with me.

Leslie Chauncey, Kaye Saunders, Jennifer Potts, Anne Sena, Caren Keefe, Jill Jennings, Isabel Taylor, Deana Merrell, Rachel Franke, Susi Gott Seguret, Debra Sarbaugh, Kristi Hampton, Mary Weaver: For the love and the unique way each one of you have been my behind-the-scenes amazing support!

My teachers, whose presence and dedication to transformation have ignited my journey: Jack Canfield, Louise Hay, Wayne Dyer, Nancy Levin,

Patricia Crane, Rick Nichols, Rick Moss, Mike Dooley, and SARK: Thank you for bringing form to my visions and helping to ignite the courageous lion within.

My Mighty Mermaids group: For teaching me to own my leadership role and for joining a tribe that believes in true transformation and silly celebrations.

To all the people who openly shared their stories: For your courage to rewrite old stories and design your transformative new stories. I applaud you. Know that your journey is sure to inspire others.

My clients: Who trust me to hold the mirror for them to step into their greatness and experience life with the knowledge that they truly are enough already. I'm honored to be a part of your journey.

To God and all my amazing behind-the-scene angel helpers: I am forever grateful! And, I am doing the happy dance!!

CPSIA information can be obtained
at www.ICGtesting.com
Printed in the USA
BVHW031535291118
534326BV00002B/11/P